HISTORIANS, BOOKS AND LIBRARIES

Historians
Books
and
Libraries

A Survey of Historical Scholarship

in Relation to Library Resources,

Organization and Services

By Jesse Hauk Shera

Dean of the School of Library Science

Western Reserve University

GREENWOOD PRESS, PUBLISHERS
NEW YORK

CONTENTS

FOREWORD

Dr. Shera, Director of the School of Library Science at Western Reserve University, in this volume presents further proof, if proof were needed, of the close affinity that exists among historians and librarians. Though primarily designed to make librarians more aware of the world of historical scholarship and the historian's demands upon the resources and services of a well-administered library, this study will prove of value also to students of history who need to realize the importance of the most essential tool of their craft, and learn to use it to greater advantage.

History at best is what the social memory has preserved of what occurred years and centuries ago. It remains a barren, meaningless chronicle, unless historians, specially trained for their delicate task, can provide an honest and intelligent interpretation of the so-called facts of history. Both the materials upon which their conclusions are based, and the needs, experiences and plans for the future, are likely to change, as each age weaves its own logic into the pattern of the past. History is constantly being re-written, in terms of what its proper scope and social purpose should be.

The librarian is the keeper of the priceless records that have survived the ravages of time, and from which the historian must re-construct the past and try to give it meaning. Every historical scholar knows the importance of a good system of private librarianship for himself, and he knows still better how the services of a good library can facilitate and speed his research. Thus, anything that enables librarians and historians to understand each other better, is a welcome addition to one's knowledge of the functions and techniques of these two important groups. One of the specific purposes of this volume is to bring about a closer rapprochement in this area of creative scholarship.

Both undergraduate and graduate students can profit from a study of this essay in mutual understanding and cooperative service of two great professions. Dr. Shera has summarized, in compact form, the major trends in the changing concepts of history from ancient times to the present. He has explained how historical materials generally are arranged in libraries, and he has given a summary of the various types of reference materials essential to historical reading and research, as well as a general statement of several kinds of historical scholarship and the way historians, in each case, use the material available. In short, here is an attempt, and I think a successful one, to present a pattern of the ways in which an historian works, the kind of sources he needs and uses, their relative value in connection with his special problem, and what a good library can do to aid him in his work.

Librarians and historians, if they will read and reflect upon the problem presented here, will understand each other better, and learn much about each other's responsibility in a cooperative undertaking to produce better history, and to generate greater interest in the reading and study of history.

Carl Wittke

Western Reserve University

AUTHOR'S INTRODUCTION

In 1945 when Ralph A. Beals, now Director of the New York Public Library, was appointed Dean of the Graduate Library School of the University of Chicago, he and the present writer began seriously to discuss the curriculum of the library school and the possibilities for reorganization and improvement. Both were dissatisfied with the traditional courses in "book selection," in which the student was, presumably taught to evaluate library materials in terms of their potential use for a wide variety of purposes. Both were also of the opinion, then but vaguely and uncertainly expressed, that it would be possible to substitute for the traditional "book selection" course a course, or sequence of courses, that would approach the problem of developing the library's book collection in terms of the major academic areas -- the social sciences, the physical sciences, and the humanities -- rather than from the point of view of the library procedures and techniques involved. But such a course, or courses, would not be limited to the evaluation of library materials, but would unite in a single comprehensive whole the totality of basic library operations in cataloging, classification, acquisition, selection, and reference so that the student could comprehend them as an integrated unity in which each part made its particular contribution to the success of the library as an effective agency for the dissemination of recorded information.

Some preliminary experimentation with such a course was carried out during the academic year 1945-46, but it was not until the autumn of 1946, with the appointment to the faculty of the Graduate Library School of Margaret E. Egan, that a really serious attack upon the problem was begun. Miss Egan not only accepted the basic premises of Beals and Shera, but to their thinking she contributed an insistence upon the importance of use of library materials. It was her belief that in every situation involving books and people the librarian must bring to bear a body of knowledge, a point of view, and a set of skills which, taken together, are the peculiar possession of the professional librarian and are the tools with which he must work, whatever his level of operation must be. Older generations of librarians had acquired this professional equipment through long years of daily experience and observation, often without full awareness of the many factors which made the resulting knowledge and skills different in kind from the somewhat similar knowledge and skills of the scholar, the teacher, or the avid "general reader." The librarian, therefore, must have some knowledge of books and some knowledge of people, but the central point upon which his attention must <u>always</u> focus is the <u>relationship between books</u>

and people -- how different kinds of people use different kinds of books for different kinds of purposes. Such a course must, therefore, center about the substantive content of library materials and the critical estimate of their intrinsic worth, but it must also thoroughly familiarize the student with the totality of equipment, both physical and intellectual, that librarians have devised to facilitate this relationship between recorded information and those who use, or should use, it. Further, it is the responsibility of the library school, as well as of the profession of librarianship, to examine and revise constantly this equipment in the light of evolving patterns of need and use.

Accordingly, during the winter quarter of the year 1947-48, such a course for the major disciplines of the social sciences, and under the direction of Miss Egan, was inaugurated at the Graduate Library School. In this course, history, for which the present writer was made responsible, received major emphasis inasmuch as it is one of the most important subject fields with which the librarian is concerned. The present text, therefore, in spite of the fact that it represents a long period of discussion and instruction is, even in its present form, still a frankly experimental attempt to provide integrated training and practice in the several types of knowledge and skills which the librarian must use in dealing with historical writing in its many forms. That this experimentation, not only in history but in the other major academic disciplines, will be continued at the School of Library Science at Western Reserve University is the expectation of the present writer.

This text may, therefore, be properly regarded as a preliminary sampling of the kind of instructional material that will eventually be developed at the School of Library Science after the completion of the proposed curriculum study here makes more clearly discernible the textual materials that such an advanced curriculum will demand. If it does not answer all of the questions concerning the nature of the "core curriculum" of the library school, at least it may be of some service in making more clear to the profession the direction which the present writer believes future education for librarianship should follow.

To the Student

To achieve the proper integration between the substantive content of historical writings and the uses to which they are put by the several types of library patrons, it is desirable that the student work out certain appropriate exercises, as may be devised by the instructor, at the same time that he is studying the text. The three following exercises, prepared by Miss Egan, have been tested by her in actual classroom situations and may be of demonstrative value.

Exercise I

In order to provide practice in the close analysis of a book according to the criteria developed in the text it is desirable that all students read the same title in at least one instance.   There are a number of suitable titles now available in paper-back reprints, which are so inexpensive that each student may be asked to buy his own copy to be marked or cut up as he sees fit.   Gordon Childe's What Happened in History has been used for this purpose with considerable success, illustrating as it does a variety of types of evidence used and several easily discerned concepts and theories borrowed from other disciplines.   Whatever title is chosen, the student should read it with questions such as the following in mind and class discussion should center around these or similar appropriate points:

1.   If the introduction or the first chapter states explicitly the purpose of the author does such a statement enable the reader to "place" the book in relation to a particular school of historical writing or to a particular point of view concerning history or society?

2.   If the purpose of the author is not explicitly stated, is it possible to infer such purpose from the contents?   Does either the first or the last chapter summarize the author's hypotheses or conclusions? Are there summary paragraphs at the end of each chapter which give a quick view of the author's conclusions?

3.   If there are no easily found statements within the text, does the table of contents throw any light upon the scope of the author's treatment or the aspects of the problem which seem important to him?

4.   What kinds of evidence has he used?   Does he indicate how he established the authenticity or reliability of his evidence?   Has he used primary or secondary sources, or both?   Can you think of any type of evidence which he might have used but has not?

5.   Has he borrowed the point of view, the concepts, the theories, or the methods of any discipline other than history?   If so, what? Has he over-extended the significance or the certainty of such borrowings?   For instance, in the title mentioned above Childe suggests as a reason for the downfall of certain early communities a failure in economic distribution -- the inability to provide an income adequate for the consumption of the local product.   This is so close to Keynesian doctrine that one might well question whether or not Childe is using a theory as an established fact or whether his findings tend to substantiate the argument of Keynes.   To answer such a question requires a critical knowledge of economics which the librarian may not be reasonably expected to have.   This is the point at which the librarian should have recourse to reviews, and to have such specific questions in mind will help him to use reviews intelligently.   In this case reviews of both Childe's and Keynes' books might be used.   Certainly, reviews published in economic journals would be most likely to be helpful.

6. What educational level must a reader have reached in order to read the book with comprehension and enjoyment? Is the book likely to be read only by those who will be able to criticize it or is it likely to appeal to readers who habitually accept anything the author says? It is in the latter case, of course, that the librarian must exercise greatest care; the mature and critical reader may be safely left to carry on his own argument with the author.

7. If it is possible to estimate the range of reader appeal the book will have, for what type of library is this volume a suitable purchase?

If this analysis is carried on as a class exercise, the student may be expected to use the same approach, although obviously not with the same thoroughness, when he inspects the volumes assembled for Exercise II.

Exercise II

There is a definite limit to the number of volumes which a librarian can read completely and analytically. Certainly the student who is attempting to survey the literature of a complete field in a few weeks can not be expected to read many illustrative titles, although it is desirable for him to read at least two or three if he can. The student, however, like the librarian at work, will have to depend upon quick but systematic inspection of a large number of titles in order to extend his working knowledge of books. Because the evaluation of books includes noting the same facts about author, publisher, physical features, and contents as are needed in classifying and cataloging there is economy of time and concentration of attention in combining practice in these operations.

A number of the titles cited in the text to illustrate historical writing of a certain type, period, or school will be assembled in the library (or laboratory) for the convenience of the student. The titles listed at the end of the chapters, chosen to illustrate special problems in cataloging or classifying as well as types of publications, are suggested as a desirable collection for such practice work. Whenever possible, inexpensive modern editions (sometimes chosen to represent series with which the student should become familiar) have been listed. Old and rare volumes might better be shown and talked about in class in order to avoid unnecessary wear. Other editions may be substituted for the titles listed or other titles may be selected. In any case the student should work with the books at the time he is reading the appropriate part of the text. Note that the titles are grouped and chapter headings from the text indicated in order to make easy reference possible.

Instructions:

A. Examine each book carefully, noting facts of authorship, publication, and physical format. How many of the questions asked about Childe's What Happened in History could you answer about this book without reading it completely? What

evidence can you find in the book itself that is of the type discussed in the part of the text where it is cited? Do you think
you could discern similar characteristics if you came across
them in a book which was completely unknown to you?

B. Write annotations (not to exceed a hundred words) of six titles
of your own choice, disregarding groupings. Three of your
annotations should be designed for staff use only, stating the
qualifications of the title for library use, and the other three
should be descriptive notes intended to induce readers to ask
for the book.

C. Classify and catalog one title from each group, making the main
entry card only but indicating tracings. Select for this purpose
books which illustrate different kinds of cataloging problems or
practices. Use such manuals as Dewey, Sears, ALA Cataloging
Rules, and Mann to solve as many as possible of the problems
you encounter. If you can not find the proper procedure raise
the question for class discussion.

Exercise III

Each of the titles indented in the body of the text is to be inspected
with some care. Examine the scope, arrangement, and special features
of each, but consider each as an example of a type rather than as an outstandingly important reference tool in itself. Do you know, or can you
find, others like it? Would you know where to look for a similar volume?
From your inspection of each title formulate a question which could be
more fully or more easily answered from that source than from any other
with which you may be familiar.
Answers to some, but not all, of the following questions can be
found in the volumes to be inspected. If you do not find the answers in
the course of your assigned reading and inspection, try some of the general aids to reference work with which you are already familiar or which
you may locate through Mudge, Winchell, Shores, Hirshberg, etc. The
purpose of this exercise is to give practice in the analysis of questions,
to give some motivation to systematic inspection, and to provide a basis
for class discussion. If you find that you are spending too much time on
a question, drop it and ask for a class discussion.

Sample Questions

1. Can you suggest any novels set in Britain during the period of the
Roman occupation?

2. When, and between what countries, was the War of Jenkins' Ear
fought?

3. Can you suggest two or three films showing colonial life in New England which would be suitable for fifth or sixth grade children?

4. In what libraries of the Southeast are there good genealogical collections?

5. Has a history of the county in which you were born ever been published?

6. Who began the movement for the Children's Crusade?

7. Find the name of the leading newspaper published in Sacramento. Is it available on microfilm? Where is the nearest file? Is there an index to it anywhere?

8. What was the name of the first American to enter Japan as an official representative of the United States government?

9. Which baseball teams contended for the World Series title when you were ten years old? Upon what date did the Series open in that year?

10. Who was "Typhoid Mary?"

11. Which of the sources known to you (including the card catalog) gives the best list of titles on sigillography?

12. Where might one find information as to what, if any, diplomatic measures were taken before the United States went to war with the Barbary pirates?

13. Can you suggest titles of books giving authentic pictures of home life in thirteenth century France?

14. Where can you find a complete list of the men who have served on the bench of the United States Supreme Court?

15. What well-known literary figures were contemporaneous with Erasmus? How might you get a complete list of those with whom he corresponded?

16. On what day of the week did February 8th fall in 1836?

17. How much is known about the life of Alcuin?

18. What was the origin of May Day?

19. When was the modern calendar established, and by what authority did it become international?

20. What were the social or economic conditions which made the people of Argentina ready to accept a dictator?

Perhaps the most efficient procedure is to examine the exercises before the reading of the text is begun, then returning to the exercises as each chapter is completed. The inspection, cataloging, classifying, and annotating of each of the titles selected, and the thorough examination of each of the reference tools cited in the body of the text to determine the reference questions it will answer and the other uses to which it might be put will familiarize the student not only with the substantive content of the materials, but will place them in their proper setting in the work of the librarian. The re-reading of the appropriate portions of the text as titles are examined and exercises prepared will also prove helpful in the assimilation of the course content. Through the use of such a procedure both textual material and library operations will assume greater meaning and be more easily mastered than is likely if the exercises are postponed until the completion of the reading of the entire text.

Acknowledgements

My very heavy obligation to both Ralph A. Beals and Margaret E. Egan is implicit throughout the above paragraphs, without their substantial assistance this text could probably not have been written, certainly it could not have attained whatever success it may achieve. My debt to both is very great indeed.

But others have also contributed generously to the content of this work. Donald M. Dozer of the U. S. Department of State and Philip D. Jordan of the Department of History of the University of Minnesota read the manuscript with great care and made many helpful criticisms. The late Pierce Butler, Professor Emeritus of the Graduate Library School, and Clarence Faust of the Ford Foundation, made particularly helpful suggestions concerning the earlier chapters. To Carl Wittke, Dean of the Graduate School of Western Reserve University, I am deeply indebted not only for a careful reading of the text but for his very thoughtful introduction. Helen M. Focke of the faculty of the School of Library Science of Western Reserve, and Helen R. Sattley, formerly of the same faculty and now Director of School Libraries for the City of New York, both gave generously of their rich experience in teaching in this field.

Ralph R. Shaw, Librarian of the U. S. Department of Agriculture, not only read the manuscript with care and made many helpful suggestions, but he graciously waived a prior claim to the publication of the manuscript by the Scarecrow Press so that it might appear under the imprint of Western Reserve University.

Howard Allen, University Editor, and Director of the Western Reserve University Press, has been most cooperative in every possible way, and Margaret Kaltenbach, Registrar of the School of Library Science, has spared no effort to see the manuscript through the press. Finally, my wife, Helen B. Shera has, as always, not only improved the literary style, but deepened and enriched its intellectual content.

One customarily concludes such a preliminary statement with an expression of relief that a long task has reached its conclusion, but in this instance we can only express the hope that the work has just begun.

School of Library Science   Jesse H. Shera
Western Reserve University
June 14, 1953

CHAPTER 1

INTRODUCTION: THE LIBRARY AND HISTORY

History, which is quite generally accepted as one of the social sciences today and is so treated here, actually stands at a transitional point between the social sciences and the humanities, serving as a bridge between the two. As a distinctive intellectual interest history, whether it be considered art or science, antedates by many centuries those branches of social thought which have separated themselves from philosophy within the past two centuries. The walls of Egyptian tombs were covered with historical records of the exploits of national rulers and heroes; the Greeks gave to Clio a place among the Muses.

This universal interest of man in his past gave the initial impetus to the establishment of libraries, and the history of the library as an institution will be considered here, together with a general treatment of the problems, methods, and development of historical research. The history of libraries may be seen as a proper field of research by librarians, inasmuch as they are the logical historians of their own professional activities.

From the clay tablets of Ashurbanipal and the papyri of the Pharaohs to the microcards of Fremont Rider the historical thread has been conspicuous in the pattern of library formation and development. An awareness of the need to preserve the record of past experiences and a desire to perpetuate for posterity the achievements of the present were the dominant motives which were responsible for the formation of the libraries of the ancient world. Even today the great national libraries, the British Museum, the Bibliothèque Nationale, the Library of Congress are still dominantly conservational.

The movement for the widespread establishment of public libraries in the United States owes a substantial debt to those professional historians who pressed for repositories in which they might find the books they needed to pursue their own studies, and to the countless local antiquarians who sought to preserve for future generations the modest records of their own communities. So strong has been this historical consciousness, not to say conscientiousness, that there have been those who have argued that it has been a deterrent to the development of an adequate library service. On the other hand, the public library, to a far greater extent than the great national or research libraries, has been responsible for the widespread dissemination of the products of historical scholarship. It has been a major agency in making operative in contemporary society whatever understanding or insights history has to offer.

Unlike the other social sciences, most of which have arisen when certain phases of man's activities have become so complex that they have developed specialized social organizations and methods, history covers all of man's activities. There are no particular social agencies the activities of which provide the raw materials of history or which might be used to implement directly the conclusions or recommendations of the historian. Obviously, then, there are no special groups of technologists or administrators to require special library services in history. Knowledge of history can have practical social value only when individual citizens in their many separate spheres of interest are guided in their judgments, decisions, and actions by a disciplined awareness of the experience of the past. The concern of librarians, therefore, is to provide library facilities for those scholars engaged in the writing of history, for educators and students at all levels, and for members of the general public.

CHAPTER II

THE SCHOLAR AND HISTORY

The Scope and Problems of History

Definition and Value

History, according to Carl Becker, is "the knowledge of things said and done." More precisely, it is the record of past human action. In brief, the historian is a general social scientist whose primary concern is with the past. In the pursuit of his inquiry the historian may proceed as a political scientist, a sociologist, an economist, a psychologist, but always he begins with a knowledge of his own ignorance, a question to which he seeks the answer. He is not content to record that which is already known or to rearrange data in new patterns unless by so doing he can make a substantial contribution to the sum of human knowledge.

But the true historian does not set out to discover new facts or to point out new relationships for the mere sport of the chase; such activities may be safely left to the antiquarian. The objective of history is human self-knowledge, and its value is that it teaches us what man has done and therefore what man is. The cynicism that "Man learns nothing from history except that he learns nothing from history," is only a half-truth, for man has learned much from history even though he has not always learned as much as he should. There is ample evidence that those who are determined to remain ignorant of history are destined to repeat its errors. Perhaps R. G. Collingwood has best stated the case for the value of history:

> It is generally thought to be of importance to man that he should know himself, where knowing himself means knowing not merely personal peculiarities . . . but his nature as man. Knowing yourself means knowing, first, what it is to be a man; secondly, knowing what it is to be the kind of man you are; and thirdly, knowing what it is to be the man you are and nobody else is. Knowing yourself means knowing what you can do; and since nobody knows what he can do until he tries, the only clue to what man can do is what man has done. The value of history, then, is that it teaches us what man has done and thus what man is. [1]

---

[1]
R. G. Collingwood. The Idea of History. (Oxford: The Clarendon Press, 1946), p. 10.

History, then, is not an empty and sterile antiquarianism pursued for its own sake and for the thrill of discovery, but rather a search through the record of human thought and actions for a better understanding of society and the individual's relation to society. In short, the historian is the sociologist of the past, whose basic intent is so to reconstruct history that it will present an intelligible record which will enable man better to understand his nature as a social being.

Point of View

But no historian can possibly present all the details of even a small segment of the past. Each must "pick and choose" from among the data available to him; he must, of necessity, select those phenomena which to him seem relatively most important for his purpose. This implies, then, that the historian is always writing with a purpose, and that his selection is related to the general ideas or underlying philosophy to which he is committed. His basic ideas or beliefs, whether expressed or implied, will always exhibit themselves in his selection of the segments of the past with which he chooses to deal, his choice of the events which he elects to narrate, his emphases in the characterization of his subjects, his interpretation of the changes which his history traces. Few historians are content merely to set down facts in isolation, but quite properly the historian seeks to establish causal explanations of what has taken place, and his postulation of causality is a further expression of, and indeed a commitment to, his underlying ideas and beliefs. In this sense, then, all history is biased, for the historian must of necessity select this rather than that aspect of the events with which he deals, and propose this rather than that causal explanation of them. In these choices and in the historian's underlying philosophy there exists a reciprocal relationship, each in measure determining the other. History is not a simple photographic negative on the sensitive surface of which is recorded every minute detail of light and shadow to which it has been exposed. Rather, there is always a point of view, an "angle", a distortion, if one chooses so to call it, that is determined by the predispositions of the photographer-historian. But these very deviations from precise representation may well give to the "photograph" more meaning than would be derived from simple delineation.

This limitation is not a handicap to history, for the value of historical writing often derives from this point of view, these insights, which the historian brings to bear upon the chaos of the past, just as the artistic meaning of a photograph is more dependent upon the skill of the photographer in the suppression or emphasis of the constituent parts of his picture than upon the precise representation of unselected detail. Bias and distortion are injurious to history when they result in the suppression and elimination of elements which, in terms of its own principles of selection, characterization, and causation, should not be disregarded, or when it prompts the author to make positive statements or conclusions that are not justified by the available data.

4

Types of History

The need for selectivity in the writing of history has, in turn, given rise to a wide variety in the kinds of history that have been produced. These types may be perceived and classified in terms of (a) the ends which historians have wished to serve; (b) the several subject areas they have elected to examine; and (c) the variety of methods they have chosen to employ: -

(a) By purpose:

The purpose of the historian may be purely descriptive, a simple narration of events without interpretation or synthesis, set down in chronological order as they took place, or recounted in retrospect from the memory of the writer, or organized in any other convenient form. Typical of such history are the chronicles or annals, such as the Anglo-Saxon Chronicle, or the city chronicles of Nuremberg or Cologne. The diary and the journal are highly personalized variants of this same genre. But even in this rather primitive type of history the narration of events is often subordinate to other ends. The Magdeburg Centuries was essentially a Protestant attack upon the authority of the Roman Catholic Church, and the Annales Ecclesiastici was the Catholic answer. Certainly the Anglo-Saxon Chronicle does not give a sympathetic picture of the Danes. The most conscientious annalist finds it difficult to set down a chronology of isolated, particular events without comment, evaluation, or causal explanation. Though much of our local history is annalistic in form, personal or community pride is so potent an influence that much of it is factually unreliable.

To the librarian, especially the reference librarian, descriptive or narrative history, when its authenticity has been established, is extremely important, especially when it takes the form of factual compilations such as:

Langer, William Leonard, ed. An Encyclopedia of World History, Ancient, Medieval and Modern, Chronologically Arranged. A rev. and modernized version of Ploetz's "Epitome." Boston: Houghton Mifflin Company, 1948. 1270 pp.

Dictionary of American History James Truslow Adams, ed. in chief. 2d ed., rev. New York: Scribner, 1942. 5 v. and index.

But many historians are not content merely to record events, piling them one upon the other without regard to their interrelationships. They interject into the narrative observations as to possible causal relationships in an attempt to make such events intelligible as aspects or expressions of the peculiar quality of an age, of a society, or of an individual. History then becomes interpretative in purpose. Examples of this are so common as to make illustration superfluous. As has been shown above, even descriptive history can be, and indeed is, interpretative to a limited degree. Such interpretation opens the door to subjective appraisal -- which after all is not an improper function of the historian, for if he himself does not glean wisdom from his studies, how can the reader be expected to do so?

The librarian, like every other user of historical writings, must know the nature of this interpretation, the predispositions of the author that direct his choices, and the limitations imposed upon the author by external factors. In short, he must know that Cotton Mather interpreted American history in terms of the manifestation of Divine Destiny; that George Bancroft saw the Revolution as the spontaneous uprising of a free and democratic people against tyranny and oppression; that Frederick Jackson Turner treated the interaction of the West with the East as our major cultural determinant; that to Charles A. Beard American history was shaped by the conflict among antagonistic economic interests; and that Arthur Schlesinger emphasized the growing importance of the "common man". If the librarian is unaware of the importance of interpretation to historical writing, or is ignorant of the forms in which it may manifest itself, he can scarcely hope to select his book-stock intelligently or to recommend titles to his patrons with discretion and judgment. In this task the traditional library tools will be of small help; the card catalogue, the book classification, the standard subject-heading lists were not constructed to supply this kind of bibliographic aid. Although book reviews will be of some assistance, there is no substitute for a thorough understanding of the course of historiography, the major outlines of which can be only suggested in the following pages.

"Schools of thought" in historical writing are largely determined by the nature of the interpretation that marks them. While it is easy to overemphasize those qualities that distinguish one from the others, a general awareness of the factors characteristic of each school will simplify the task of the librarian in evaluating historical materials.

Historical writing may also serve a third purpose, that of justifying or condemning individuals, social groups, nations, or civilizations. In such evaluative history the details of the past are marshalled for the purpose of supporting moral judgments or partisan viewpoints. Contrast, for example, William Bradford's account of the goings-on at Merrymount, in 1628, with that given by one of the chief participants, Thomas Morton, in his New English Canaan. Again one may see this same phenomenon operating in the accounts of the Battle of Lake Champlain, as presented in the history texts for American and Canadian secondary schools -- so strongly nationalistic are these treatments that each side insists that its own forces were seriously outnumbered by the enemy.[2] Likewise one has but to recall

---

2
    For a full treatment of the subject of national bias in school textbooks see Arthur Walworth, School Histories at War. (Cambridge: Harvard Univ. Press, 1938). 92 pp.

those crowded years from 1933 to 1945 to realize the evaluative task confronting historians in assessing the true character of Franklin D. Roosevelt from such divergent accounts as those presented in Frances Perkins' The Roosevelt I Knew, Eleanor Roosevelt's This I Remember, Robert E. Sherwood's Roosevelt and Hopkins, James A. Farley's Jim Farley's Story: The Roosevelt Years, and John T. Flynn's Country Squire in the White House.

Finally, the historian may so order his narrative of the past as to make of it a chart and a practical guide for the future. In the writing of such practical history a knowledge of the past is sought as a basis for right action in the present or the planning of policies for the future. Such practical history is not essentially different from interpretative history, except that as a type it is frequently more limited in its subject matter. Histories of particular institutions, such as the Tennessee Valley Authority, or the public libraries in the United States, or labor-management relations in a given industry, are good examples of the kind of history that may serve as a guide to practical action.

The purposes which motivate historians are not isolated, discrete forces which operate singly and alone but, more frequently, exist in combination and in varying proportion in the writings of any particular individual at any given time. Differences in purpose cut across, and in large measure determine, another set of distinctions which relate to the subject matter selected by the historian, and to the methods by which he works.

(b) By subject:

The historian may thus regard as the dynamic subject matter of his history nations, social groups, economic classes, religious denominations, institutions, individuals or even such abstract forces or ideas as commercialism, mercantilism, rationalism, liberalism, democracy, or totalitarianism. Similarly, all disciplines and branches of knowledge may be in themselves the subject matter of history. Thus, there is the history of science, or any branch thereof, the history of literature, the history of librarianship, linguistic history, and the like. In characterizing any of these agents the historian may become preoccupied with, or at least emphasize, certain traits or attributes of his subject, such as the physical, the psychological, the ethical, the social, or the economic. This choice of agents and of the traits to be emphasized is closely related to the kind of interpretation chosen and, with it, determines the "historical school," or "school of thought" to which a historian is said to belong. So also, the development of disciplines other than history prepared the way for future historians to initiate new schools of thought by making possible the discovery of new agents in history and new traits to be emphasized, thus giving rise to new hypotheses as to historical causation.

(c) By method:

7

From these other disciplines, as well as from historical scholarship, emerge new methods or variations in method which constitute a third basis for differentiation among historians. New methods may lead to the discovery of new facts as well as to the reassessment of old data. Thus method, like purpose and subject matter, contributes to placing the historian in the school with which he is associated. The same subject matter, dealt with for the same purpose, may be subjected to different methods of clarification, interpretation, and presentation.[3] One historian may be content with the "common sense" insights into the connection between human propensities and human action, while another may believe it necessary to attempt a retrospective psychoanalysis of historical characters.

One of the most striking developments in historical method has been the adoption by historians of the statistical techniques and of the theory of probability devised primarily for use in contemporary social research. The biological sciences, too, have made extensive use of statistical methods, and the work of R. A. Fisher and others at Rothamstead did much to refine the processes of statistics for the social scientist. The historian of the future will certainly depend increasingly upon the reliable quantitative descriptions compiled by the statisticians of today.

Finally, there are historians who cross over into the humanities to borrow the techniques of imaginative reconstruction of the past. Such historians feel quite justified in fabricating conversations of which there could be no "primary" record, in elaborating imagined accounts of action, or even in reconstructing the thought processes of historical personages. Imaginative history is not arbitrarily to be condemned as either inaccurate or intellectually dishonest. When skillfully used, and supported by a skeleton of substantiated fact, this method fully justifies the claims of its adherents. It not only adds much to the vivid reconstruction of the past, but carries an emotional impact that may be lacking in a strictly factual account. From it arises the ever-popular historical novel, which, at its best, can be fully as illuminating as a textbook on formal history.

The Methods of the Historian

On the whole it may be said that the methods of the historian are identical with the methods of the other social sciences insofar as these methods can be applied to past phenomena. The methods of historical investigations are circumscribed only by the limitation that history is concerned with the past. This means that the historian must always

---

3

Exact methodological procedures are more fully dealt with in the following section "Methods," and the development of new methods from new insights or points of view are treated throughout the various period sections.

8

obtain his experiences vicariously, his methods must always be <u>indi-rect</u>. He cannot, therefore, use the <u>direct</u> methods often available to to his colleagues in the other social science fields. Except for that limitation, and it is a serious one, his methods may be co-extensive with theirs.

Regardless of particular schools of thought, there is a core of methodology common to all historians. Basically the historical method is a system of reasoning whereby the historian proceeds from the inspection and study of records (or evidence) to an understanding of facts or relationships relevant to the period or problem he is investi-gating. This interpretation of <u>graphic record</u> is the focal point of his-torical investigation; the records themselves, either documentary or artifactual, are its <u>materia historica</u>; and the library, archive, or museum, is its laboratory. The historian's data are selected for him by the very fact of their survival; he cannot choose and shape his ma-terials to the extent possible to his colleague who is studying contem-porary social phenomena. He is never able to examine all the record, however relevant or important it may be, but only that residue which has withstood the passage of time. Hence the historian has a vital stake in the preservation of records, and in the encouragement and promotion of libraries, archives, and museums.

Moreover, because the tradition is widely accepted among histo-rians that no generalization should be advanced unless all the avail-able evidence has been examined, no stone left unturned, every wit-ness summoned, they have urged the preservation of not only the more important records but the indiscriminate preservation of every-thing. Thus has emerged the custodial function of librarianship, the conviction that library collections must be complete, or as nearly com-plete as human endeavor and limited resources make possible, and the tradition that every scrap of record will eventually be important to someone. As the historian has expanded his interests to include social history in the broadest sense, and has become concerned with "grass roots" history and the contribution of the "common man" to the shaping of historical forces, the urge for comprehensive preser-vation has increased to the point that even last week's auction hand-bill becomes a document of potential historical importance.

In the past there have been just enough examples of the value of this omnivorous collecting to give the argument substantial weight, but as the more truly scientific procedures of historical method devel-op, and as the discipline itself matures, the historian should, indeed must, learn more about the application of sampling to historical prob-lems and thus not only increase his skill in the manipulation of large masses of historical record, but abandon the false and impossible goal of "completeness." One has but to examine casually the growth of our National Archives during the past decade to be convinced of the futility of attempting to apply the procedures previously devised for historical investigation in an age when records were relatively scarce to a situation in which the remains are excessively abundant.

Auxiliary Sciences

As the nature of historical research has grown increasingly complex, and the phenomena with which it deals more specialized, certain auxiliary sciences have been developed to support it, and the assistance of related sciences has been sought. Each has evolved its own techniques and methods for the recording and preservation of its data and the interpretation of its findings. Several have evolved separate bodies of literature, including manuals, handbooks and bibliographies. The auxiliary sciences with their Dewey class numbers, which illustrate the scattering of the contributory literature, are

(a) Archaeology	571
(b) Epigraphy	417
(c) Paleography	417
(d) Sphragistics or Sigillography	320.18
(e) Numismatics	737
(f) Philately	383.22
(g) Genealogy	929.1
(h) Heraldry	929.6
(i) Chronology	529
(j) Diplomatics	421.7

(a) Archaeology:

The first of the auxiliary sciences is archaeology, the study of primitive and ancient civilizations through examination of their remains. It is basically history and its scope of interest is the same as that of history, but its available data are much more limited. Its primary materials are artifacts rather than graphic records, and these, grubbed from the debris of long-vanished communities, discovered in the luxurious tombs of Thebes, or found in the temples and public places of Greece, Rome, or Cuzco, have built up a surprisingly extensive body of knowledge concerning manufactures, commerce, customs, art, religion, and the daily life of civilizations and societies for which almost no other record has survived. The museum is second only in importance to the field of excavation for the effective work of the archaeologist. As these artifacts are brought to light and taken from an environment which was frequently almost perfect for preservation, their deterioration is rapid, so that minute description, precise measurement, and careful photography are essential if the research of the present is to be perpetuated.

The graphic record of the work then becomes even more meaningful to the investigator than the actual object itself, and in time the organization of library and bibliographic procedures for its efficient utilization will be more important than museum display. Such graphic records, in the form of photographs with attached precise descriptions of single objects, pose a problem in organization which is essentially

different from that of the record in book form. This is not merely a
difference in form and size, but a difference in habits of approach by
the potential users, for these records have then become the primary
data of research and must be approached through the properties which
are relevant to research hypotheses. It is therefore obvious that any
classification system must be special rather than general, that it must
reflect the research interests of the particular group at the particular
time, and that it must be sufficiently flexible to permit the incorporation of new categories developed by new hypotheses.

There is a large and constantly growing body of literature in book
form, which is generally classified according to one of the standard
bibliothecal systems. In Dewey, the literature of archaeology is widely dispersed; the techniques of archaeology as a science are found in
571, together with those other sciences, such as anthropology, which
are subsumed under biology; descriptions of particular excavation sites
and the objects found there are classed with other books of geography
and travel of the locality in 913-919; historical narrative derived from
such investigation is found in history, 930-999. Books which discuss
particular aspects, such as art, architecture, textiles, ceramics,
trade and industry, etc., are classified with the particular subject.
Biblical archaeology is classed with religion in 220.93; Old Testament
archaeology is in 221.931.

Bibliographic guides may be comprehensive in their treatment of
archaeology as a general discipline or they may be restricted to the
primitive history of a particular locality. Many general historical
guides include archaeology as part of the stream of history, and popular narratives of particular expeditions are generally included in
lists of travel books.

(b) Epigraphy:

Much of the material uncovered by the archaeologist contains written record in some form which must be deciphered if the full significance of the remains is to be wrested from them. Epigraphy is not concerned with records on paper, papyrus, or parchment; it is the study of
inscriptions engraved on metal, chiselled on stone, or moulded and
baked on clay. In historical investigation it fills the gap between artifacts and modern graphic records, and it is especially important to the
student of ancient civilizations since its materials, being so durable,
have often survived all other kinds of evidence.

(c) Paleography.

Closely associated with epigraphy is paleography, the science of
ancient handwriting. It is not concerned with the contents of documents,
per se, but with the writing, the external form of the script, and it is,
of course, essential to the study of all history preceding the invention of
printing. Paleography is the study of the morphology of written characters, the history of the styles of writing in different places and at

different times, as influenced by the materials and the instruments used. Finally, it is concerned with the development of alphabets and phonetic representation.

(d) Sphragistics or Sigillography:

Sphragistics or sigillography is the study of seals -- both the implement for making the impression and the impression itself. A seal is generally held to be a guarantee of the authenticity of the document to which it is attached, but unfortunately seals can be forged, and valid seals transferred from one document to another.

(e) Numismatics:

More familiar to the layman is the study of numismatics, which as almost everyone knows, treats of coins and the inscriptions and devices stamped upon them. What is perhaps less generally known is that the discipline also includes the study of medals and medallions. Though numismatists may be popularly regarded as practitioners of a tedious, but harmless, recreation, much about the social, cultural, and economic development of a people can be learned from its coins and the metals from which they are made. Coins and medallions are the province of the museum, not the library, but more than one librarian has found himself embarrassed with a nondescript collection of battered coins. Any librarian is likely to be questioned regarding the potential value of a "find" by a patron, and librarians generally would be well advised to inform themselves of the best sources of general information concerning the rudiments of numismatics. A widely used manual is

> Standard Catalogue of United States Coins and Currency from 1652 to Present Day. New York: Scott Stamp and Coin Company. (See latest edition.)

(f) Philately:

Of less importance to the historian but a popular hobby among the general public is philately, the study of stamps. Most public library needs may be satisfied by another Scott manual:

> Standard Postage Stamp Catalogue. New York: Scott Stamp and Coin Company. (See latest edition.)

(g) Genealogy:

Genealogy, the investigation of family pedigrees, is an invaluable aid to the historian when pursued in scholarly fashion. In recent decades genealogical records have provided data for sociologists and psychologists in studies of heredity, of social prominence, of intellectual superiority, of psychological abnormalities, etc. The literature

12

is voluminous and frequently unreliable, requiring the skill of the specialist for evaluation, and special indexes for the location of particular information. For these reasons genealogy is probably best left to the special historical library or to the large research library able to support a special department.

Yet the public has always evinced a constant and fairly widespread interest in genealogical records. Although this interest is often decried as mere vanity and is exploited by the unscrupulous upon this basis, it probably arises from a deep psychological need -- the desire of the individual to realize to the full his own identity by associating himself with his roots in the past. The most intimate social tie is always with one's own family and it may well be that the more one knows of the personalities of his ancestors the more secure he feels in the realization of his own personality. Although genealogical research is a heavy drain upon a library's resources and the search frequently seems utterly trivial, such a possible psychological function should not be too lightly dismissed. At the very least, every public library must provide guides to names, both given names and surnames, such as come on the market rather regularly and are used largely by prospective parents or by those who wish to change their names. The biographical dictionaries and directories, including Burke's "Peerage," etc., are useful for this as well as for other purposes. Many libraries cannot afford -- and, indeed, should not attempt to have large collections of family genealogies, but may well include in their collections a few of the major bibliographies and indexes, such as

U. S. Library of Congress. American and English Genealogies in the Library of Congress. 2d ed. Washington: Government Printing Office, 1919. 1270 pp.

Virkus, Frederick Adams. Abridged Compendium of American Genealogy . . . Chicago: A. N. Marquis Company, 1925-33. 5 vols.

There are a few good popular guides to the techniques and resources of genealogical research which may be placed in the hands of the interested layman or graduate student in history. The most useful of these, including chapters on town records, wills, and sources available through the National Archives and the Bureau of the Census, is:

Doane, Gilbert H. Searching for Your Ancestors. Minneapolis: University of Minnesota Press, 1948. 176 pp.

The library staff (except in the special library) cannot attempt to do such searching for patrons, but may keep a file of reliable individuals who will undertake the search for a fee.

(h) Heraldry:

13

Heraldry is the study of escutcheons, shields or shield-shaped surfaces upon which coats of arms have been depicted. Systematic heraldry dates probably from about the twelfth century; today it has no legal status or value, but in mediaeval times coats of arms were symbols of governmental power and an essential feature of feudal society. The close association of heraldry and genealogy is obvious; both have been exploited for the sake of family prestige.

(i) Chronology:

Chronology is the study of calendars and other methods of measuring and labelling time, and since time is of the essence of history, chronology is essential to valid historical investigation. The questions most frequently arising in the library relate either to historical changes in the calendar or to the perpetual calendar. Usually an encyclopedia or the World Almanac will give adequate information.

(j) Diplomatics:

Diplomatics is the study of official documents; proclamations of rulers, acts of legislatures, judicial records, charters, treaties, deeds, and registers, and the methods by which they can be identified and authenticated. It draws upon paleography, sphragistics, even heraldry. In its objective, to distinguish the genuine from the spurious, it is basic to much of the work in history, political science, and law.

Related Sciences

The related as distinct from the auxiliary sciences are those disciplines which, though not primarily concerned with historical phenomena, contribute both methodology and findings to research in history. From sociology, economics, political science, law, geography, and the other social sciences, as well as certain of the natural sciences and the humanities, the historian can learn much that will contribute greatly to the depth and richness of his own productivity. In a sense, each generation re-writes history according to its own interpretation of the past, and these interpretations are shaped not only by increasing knowledge of the facts of history, by improved techniques of historical scholarship, and by the actual findings of other disciplines, but even by the major hypotheses and theories of other disciplines. For instance, the effects of the Darwinian theory of evolution upon social thought has long been recognized; a more recent example of re-interpretation in the light of a new major theory is the use of the Keynesian hypothesis in the analysis of economic events of the past, such as Gordon Childe's in What Happened in History. [4] Further, this re-

---

4
Gordon Childe. What Happened in History. (N. Y.: Penguin Books, 1946), 280 pp. (Pelican books no. P6).

14

lationship is reciprocal since other social scientists in turn can profit from the work of the historian. All disciplines have their historical aspects, for every area of knowledge has its own history, but the relationship which we are emphasizing here is much more penetrating than that -- namely, that historical research should actually adopt, insofar as they are applicable, the methods, techniques, and procedures, as well as the findings, of the investigators in other areas of knowledge.

If the historians are to keep pace with their contemporaries in other fields they will need to be increasingly alert to developments in areas of scholarship which they have hitherto regarded as largely remote from their own. This is particularly true for those who would write library history; the library is a social agency for the transmission of whatever knowledge is available concerning social thought and action, and its own history can be interpreted adequately only in terms of its relation to the development of that knowledge. For the same reason, a knowledge of the other social sciences contributes to the librarian's ability to evaluate historical writings with respect to the social, economic, and political insights incorporated in them, an aspect as important for library purposes as their historical accuracy.

Evidence

When the historian has isolated a problem upon which he intends to work, and the point of view from which he wishes to approach it, his next step is to decide upon the types of data or evidence most likely to ensure the validity of his results. The dependence of the historian upon indirect sources of information has made the evaluation of evidence the central problem of historical research. No historical investigation can be better than the evidence upon which it is based, and though the interpretation of that evidence is a major responsibility of the historian, research supported by evidence that fails to meet the test of validity is worthless. Important as evidence is, however, one must recognize at the outset that its survival is largely fortuitous, that only within a limited range is the historian at liberty to select evidence which is most relevant to his work, and that the destruction of record is both accidental and deliberate.

One hardly needs to labor the obvious fact that our knowledge of the past has been immeasurably constricted by the action of fires, floods, and the other destructive forces of nature, the deterioration of animal and vegetable fibers and dyes, and the predatory attacks of rats, mice, and other vermin. Modern scientific methods, the use of air-conditioning with proper temperature and humidity control, the development of fungicides and germicides, the impregnation of paper with cellulose, and the improvement of photographic techniques supplemented by infra-red and ultra-violet light, have helped greatly to preserve existing records. The reconstruction of many documents hitherto thought to be practically destroyed, or at least permanently illegible, has become a reality.

15

There has also been the deliberate destruction of historical records by the premeditated actions of man himself. Much of this has been dishonest, to conceal from others information which was, or was thought to be, injurious to the interests of some individual or group, some state or nation. But the desire for secrecy is not always indicative of reprehensible motives. Every individual has the right to certain privacies and not all transactions and negotiations, both personal and public, should be generally known. The degree to which the future has a proprietory claim upon the records of the present is not always easy to determine, and when a people must choose between its own interests and those of posterity there is seldom any doubt as to which course will be followed. Finally, and this is becoming increasingly true, much is destroyed simply because its bulk makes preservation impossible. One can argue with considerable success that relatively little of real value has been lost, but it is difficult to maintain that all that has survived is worthy of preservation. Our own national and state archives are gorged with vast quantities of documentation that will never be used because they are essentially useless. The intelligent uses of sampling techniques might do much to keep such collections within manageable limits; however, it must be remembered that bases of sampling would necessarily depend upon the aspect of social or historical theory which are prevalent today, for it is as impossible for the historian as for the librarian to foresee future theories and hypotheses which the sample must document.

As has been all too aptly said, both librarians and archivists are "Collectors by instinct, selectors by chance, and rejectors, by heaven, not often!" Yet another perspicacious soul, now unhappily forgotten, has confessed to being alarmed by the growth of two phenomena in our civilization -- cemeteries and libraries -- and has suggested cremation as a solution to both. Selection in the preservation of records, then, however much one may dislike it, or however difficult the problems it raises, cannot be avoided by the librarians and historians of the future.

Types of Evidence (Primary)

a. Artifacts

Artifacts, or remains, have been widely regarded as the most reliable form of evidence because in them the subjective element is minimized. But they cannot speak for themselves; their testimony must be wrested from them by an active intelligence, which does introduce the subjective element. Furthermore, the very fact of survival may itself indicate historical insignificance or atypicality.

To take a few examples from fields of library interest, the exquisitely illuminated manuscripts of the centuries immediately preceding the invention of printing in Europe have been preserved because they were exceptional. The general impression that books of that period were all exquisite is false; the typical book of the Middle Ages was a

16

very crude and unattractive manuscript, the parchment leaves of which had probably been used more than once. Similarly the prevalence of theological treatises in many early American book collections may be implicit testimony to their relative unpopularity whereas the truly popular titles, novels, belles lettres, history, were undoubtedly worn out by heavy use and discarded in large numbers. Books, then, can have artifactual as well as substantive significance in interpreting the temper of an earlier age. Again, the proliferation of Carnegie library buildings at the turn of the present century tells us much about the struggle for culture in the late Victorian period and the part that philanthropy played in its dissemination. Other aspects of library architecture, the ubiquitous rotunda, the towers of Richardson, and especially the alcove system of book-shelving, all may have exercised a profound influence upon library organization and operation.

A variety of technological tests have been devised to establish the authenticity of the artifact, whatever its material or form. These, however, are the province of the museum curator, the archaeologist, and the anthropologist, not of the librarian, who would be well-advised to be wary of passing judgment upon anything less obvious then "the skull of John the Baptist as a boy."

b. Inscriptions

Inscriptions bridge the gap between artifacts and graphic records. Insofar as their content is restricted to factual statements of an official sort the subjective element in them is minimized. But when their content displays any trace of national or personal pride they must be subjected to the same tests of authenticity as are applied to other forms of graphic records.

c. Official Public Records

The Official public records of highly civilized countries probably more nearly approach perfect evidence than any other form of documentation. The honor of a state or nation is implicit in its laws, statutes, treaties, court records, proceedings of governing bodies, official messages of executives, and the reports of commissions and governmental agencies. Great care is taken to preserve the accuracy of these materials for vast interests are frequently at stake and even minor errors can have disastrous consequences. Further, the wealth and power of a state can command the best talent available to insure the highest possible degree of accuracy and authenticity.

Official documents are an extremely important segment of the collections of all libraries, public as well as those serving research institutions, and their importance is increasing. To the law librarian they are, of course, his stock in trade; and the growth of governmental agencies and the expansion of governmental function and responsibilities have necessitated the creation of libraries to serve these peculiar needs. So important has governmental action become for business enterprise that the special librarians serving both business and technical undertakings are in constant need of official public records of many kinds. The rapid growth in the volume of scientific and technical reports, and their great importance to industry has intensified the concern of practicing librarians in the problems and techniques of documentation. All librarians, whether they are assisting a local historian to prepare a paper for a group meeting or aiding in the research of a governmental commission or legislative body, must have some knowledge of the structure of government at the local and national levels, of the extent of governmental activities, and of the degree to which such activities are reflected in the appropriate records.

But even such records, for all the care that is taken to insure their accuracy, are not infallible. The preamble to a statute may set forth reasons for its enactment which are wholly irrelevant or untrue; the enactment of a law does not guarantee its public support or reveal the extent to which its enforcement was successful; proceedings do not always record what actually went on, for many speeches or statements may have been read only by title; official proclamations may be, and often are, wholly partisan; diplomatic documents must always be viewed with suspicion, for diplomacy and veracity are far from synonymous.

d. Official Private Records

Much of what has been said above, both positively and negatively, about official public records is also true of official private records, though here the chances for the destruction of certain types of secret information or deliberate failure to record the most important transactions is probably greater. Reasons for such secrecy may be quite legitimate, though with the increased concern of government with private enterprise the need for more meticulous procedures will tend to increase accurate private records in the future. For the librarian as well as for the historian, private records are of growing importance. Many industries and commercial enterprises are becoming increasingly aware of the value of archival collections of their own records for the efficient operations of their daily work, and others recognize a social responsibility to make their records freely available to scholarship. The Burlington Railroad has deposited its records in the Newberry Library in Chicago, and many enterprises have established or are considering the establishment of archives of their own. Thus, even the smaller public libraries may find it eventually desirable to accumulate at least a sample of the records of industry and commerce and of other private associations within their own communities.

e. Newspapers

To the historian of modern times the value of newspapers as historical evidence is second only to that of official public records. Indeed certain parts of our daily press, such as market quotations, foreign exchange, weather reports, and legal notices, have a quasi-offi-

18

cial character. In nations where the press is rigidly controlled by the government, in Russia (Pravda and Izvestia), and in Germany and Italy under Hitler and Mussolini, newspapers may be regarded as official pronouncements, but are, or course, also instruments of official propaganda. The value of the newspaper as historical evidence varies greatly from country to country, city to city, and time to time. The newspaper reached its highest development in the English-speaking countries during the nineteenth century and its value as historical source material is correspondingly greatest for that period. This is substantiated by McAnally's citation analysis in which references to newspapers issued between the years 1840-1888 account for one-half of all such citations, and more than two-thirds were dated prior to 1900. [5]

The French historian, Danau, 1842, was the first to point out the value of the newspaper to historical research, but it was John B. McMaster, in his History of the People of the United States (1883-1913), who was the first to make extensive use of the newspaper in historical investigation. Indeed this was one of his chief contributions to American historiography, and after his example no historian could afford to neglect the newspaper as an important source. [6]

Unfortunately, the day of the great editors such as Charles A. Dana, Whitelaw Reid, and William Allen White, would seem to have passed. The advent of the newspaper syndicate, the growth of the great "wire-services" -- Associated Press, United Press, and International News Service -- and the commercial exploitation of the press to the point at which the newspaper has become mainly an advertising medium carrying a certain amount of text, all have contributed to the weakening of the newspaper as a reliable source of historical evidence. In greater or less degree the press has always been biased. Throughout the first three quarters of the nineteenth century that bias was largely political and relatively easy to detect, but with the rise of our industrial economy and the growth in importance of "big business," the bias has become more economic than political and more subtle and difficult to perceive. The editorial has abandoned its position of importance on the traditional editorial page, and has suffused itself into the reporting. Editorial policies are more and more shaped by the economic interests of advertisers. The speed with which the modern newspaper is prepared and the introduction of the re-write man to expand for publication the notes of the reporter have contributed substantially to a decline in factual accuracy of the daily press.

5

Arthur M. McAnally. "Characteristics of Materials Used in Research in United States History." (Chicago: Univ. of Chicago, Graduate Library School, Unpub. Ph. D. dissertation, 1951), 185 pp.

6

William T. Hutchinson, ed. The Marcus W. Jernegan Papers in American Historiography. (Chicago: Univ. of Chicago Press, 1937), p. 133.

Despite this downward trend in reliability, the newapaper in general, and the New York Times in particular, is still one of the most important sources for the historian, and libraries are not likely soon to be relieved of the problems and responsibilities of preserving substantial files of the Times and of local papers. Physical bulk and the rapid deterioration of wood-pulp fibres have made the storage and servicing of newspapers especially burdensome and expensive. Microfilming is at present the most nearly perfect solution and the time may very soon come when bound files of newspapers will be a rarity in most libraries. Those now available on microfilm are listed in

> Association of Research Libraries. Newspapers on Microfilm, a Union Check List. Ed. by George A. Schwegemann. Philadelphia: Association of Research Libraries, Office of the Exceutive Secreatry, 1948. 176 pp.

This list includes all entries of newspapers on microfilm which had been submitted to the National Union Catalog at the time of compilation, but the number of titles microfilmed may be expected to grow rapidly. Useful lists of newspapers published in this country are

> Ayer, H. W. and Son. H. W. Ayer and Son's Directory of Newspapers and Periodicals . . . Philadelphia: H. W. Ayer and Son, 1880-   (annual)

> Brigham, Clarence S., comp. History and Bibliography of American Newspapers 1690-1820. Worcester, Mass.: American Antiquarian Society, 1947. 2 vol.

> American Newspapers, 1821-1936: A Union List of Files Available in the United States and Canada. Ed. by Winifred Gregory. New York: H. W. Wilson Company, 1937. 791 pp.

The Gregory list gives known locations of files of each title, but the holdings are not always complete and the records do not always indicate the extent of incomplete holdings. Brigham is much more complete as to titles and locations, but is of course limited to early newspapers.

The problems of newspaper use are further complicated by lack of adequate indexing, although the New York Times Index -- the only currently published index to any American newspaper -- is useful even beyond its own files, for it will often supply the date of an event for which a fuller account may then be easily found in the local newspaper. Frequently useful in the same way, although primarily intended to be a quick chronological summary of world events is

> Facts on File; A Weekly Synopsis of World Events With Cumulative Index . . . 1940 -   New York: Person's Index, Facts on File, 1940-   vol. 1-

The constant pressure for the adequate indexing of the local press places a heavy and time-consuming load upon the library staff, but most libraries do undertake a certain amount of local indexing. A guide to the existence of such indexes, which are usually maintained only on cards is:

> Ireland, Norma O., ed. Local Indexes in American Libraries; A Union List of Unpublished Indexes. Boston: Faxon Co., 1947. 221 pp.

Properly supervised and controlled such work may be an important community service; one in which the press itself has a vested interest and in the financial support of which it should share. Uncontrolled, it may easily drain time and skill from more important activities. [7]

f. Personal Sources

The term personal sources has been applied to a vast and heterogeneous agglomeration of materials in which the subjective element is both dominant and significant. Letters, diaries, memoirs, journals, autobiographical writings and reminiscences generally have the virtues and weaknesses of any form of personal testimony. Conscientious scholarship demands that such testimony be viewed with suspicion until its reliability has been proved by relentless questioning and searching cross examination. What were the author's predispositions, sympathies, and antipathies? Did he have a reputation for veracity, or was he known for "literary distortion," if not overt falsification? What were his motivations in writing -- a thesis to advance, a cause to champion, an axe to grind? Were his powers of observation apparently good, or was he known to suffer from hallucinations, illusions, prejudices, undue bias, lack of critical sense? What were his mental powers at the time? Was he too young or too old to be a good observer? Was he reporting that which was fresh in his mind or had much time elapsed between the occurrence and the recorded account? Was he speaking from direct experience or did he rely upon tradition, legend, anecdotes, heresy, gossip and other forms of anonymous statements? Was his account actually opposed to his own best interests? Upon the answers to such questions must rest the historian's final judgment as to the reliability of his witnesses. In effect the historian is applying to evidence, although much more intensively, the same criteria the librarian uses in evaluating any historical writing for library acquisition.

The Problem of Authenticity

---

[7]
Jesse H. Shera. "The Preservation of Local Illinois Newspapers." I. L. A. Record. v. 5, no. 3 (March 1952), pp. 49-52.

The problem of evidence is further complicated by the need to establish the authenticity of the record -- first, as a physical entity;
second, as to the genuineness of the authorship; and third, as to the accuracy of the text. Documents are not always what they purport to be,
and literary history is strewn with countless forgeries executed with
varying degrees of skill. Perhaps the most famous were the spurious
nineteenth century pamphlets with which T. J. Wise duped more than
one generation of bibliophiles, until the investigations of Carter and
Pollard exposed the chicanery. Modern science has contributed a number of important techniques to historical criticism of this sort. The
chemical analysis of paper, parchment, inks, and dyes, microscopic
examination of fibres that constitute the surface on which the text appears; the use of photography, often in conjunction with ultra-violet or
infra-red light for the disclosure of alterations or palimpsests; the
microscopic measurement of handwriting or print; and the study of
water-marks, all have greatly expedited the detection of anachronism or
other indications of forgery.[8]

The natural predisposition to accept at face value the overt statement of authorship has obscured many a forgery, plagiarism, or other
illegitimate use of another's work. So-called "internal evidence," the
subtle sense of style and meticulous reading of the content, is here an
important instrument in the hands of the competent historian, who also
has at his command such "external evidence" as contemporary references to the document, or the statements of earlier authorities about it.

Finally, textual criticism has developed, through years of patient
work by literary and historical scholars, an impressive body of principles through the application of which it has become less difficult to
distinguish between sound and corrupt texts, and thus to approximate
more closely the author's real words.[9] Long experience in the examination of errors by copyists and printers, the meticulous comparison
of variant texts and the construction of "genealogies" of manuscripts,
combined with a knowledge of techniques and methods of scribes and
printers has developed three basic principles to guide the historian:

8

The problem of forgeries and other forms of literary detective
work are entertainingly dealt with by Richard D. Altick in his The
Scholar Adventurers. (N. Y.: Macmillan, 1951). 338 pp.
    In an attempt to publicize the techniques of physical analysis
(Ultra-violet light, etc.) Edgar J. Goodspeed stepped out of his own
sphere, New Testament textual criticism, to write an excellent amateur detective story, The Curse in the Colophon. (Chicago: Willett,
Clarke, 1935). 259 pp.

9

An excellent popular exposition of the techniques of textual criti-
cism ("higher criticism") as applied to the Bible is to be found in
Ernest C. Colwell's What Is the Best New Testament? (Chicago:
Univ. of Chicago Press, 1952). 126 pp.

1. Preference should be given to that reading which seems to explain best the variations that have arisen.
2. Because of the natural tendency for the weary scribe or printer to simplify his work the more difficult readings are to be preferred to the simpler.
3. Preference must be given to the reading most consonant to the style and probable date of the work.

This study of the book as a physical object to establish or disprove authenticity, in conjunction with certain aspects of investigations in textual criticism, comprises the discipline of descriptive bibliography. [10] The term is an unfortunate one since it leads to considerable confusion with other and quite different forms of bibliography (enumerative, subject, national, or practical) but it has been so long hallowed by the distinguished transactions of the Bibliographical Society of London and the truly impressive work of McKerrow, Pollard, Chapman, and Greg that, despite its awkwardness, the nomenclature is not likely to change. It should be emphasized, however, that this kind of bibliography is the province of the historian or of the literary scholar, not of the librarian, who has no more responsibility for the validation of this kind of evidence than for determining the purity of the substances used by the chemist who also patronizes his library.

Types of Evidence (Secondary)

The cynicisms that "History may not repeat itself but historians repeat each other," and "To copy from one source is plagiarism but to copy from many sources is research," scarcely do justice to the value and importance of "secondary" sources in historical investigation. Failure to utilize the work of one's predecessors is not only inefficient and unscholarly, but in an age when research is becoming more and more specialized such neglect is reprehensible. The historian must take into account the work of specialists whose findings have relevance for his own results.

Traditionally, secondary sources, as distinct from primary sources, are the writings of those who have not had direct experience with the event narrated; literally, they are the reports of those who have received their information second-hand. The distinction is thoroughly conventional, artificial, and no longer very meaningful. The same work may be a primary source for one scholar and a secondary source for another. Cole's Irrepressible Conflict is certainly a secondary source for those scholars studying the origins of the Civil War, but it would be a primary source for anyone investigating the changing attitudes of American historians toward the reasons for the precipitation of that conflict.

10

R. B. McKerrow. An Introduction to Bibliography for Literature Students. (Oxford: Oxford Univ. Press, 1927). 358 pp.

The historian, therefore, uses secondary sources for : (a) general background information, (b) special types of information, particularly in areas where his own knowledge is inadequate for his purposes, (c) information not otherwise available to him, (d) assurance that the work he is doing has not already been done by others, and (e) profit from the mistakes of his predecessors.

What has been said above with reference to the validity of primary evidence is equally applicable to secondary materials, though in the latter the problem of bias is perhaps the most important. Complete objectivity is beyond the grasp of human attainment and one cannot but wonder if its realization might not prove it to be a very dull and unattractive thing indeed. The historian must take bias for granted, but he must also develop the skill to use his awareness of that bias to serve his own best interests.

Bibliography

Methods of Historical Research

Barnes, Harry Elmer. A History of Historical Writing. Norman: Univ. of Oklahoma Press, 1937.

Beard, Charles A. The Nature of the Social Sciences. N. Y.: Scribner, 1934.

Becker, Carl L. Everyman his own Historian. Am. Hist. Rev. v. 37 (1933) pp. 221-236.

Borr, Henri, and Febre, Lucien. "History and Historiography." Encyclopedia of the Social Sciences.

Collingwood, R. G. The Idea of History. Oxford: Clarendon Press, 1946.

Fox, Dixon Ryan. The Historical Essay and the Critical Review. N. Y.: Columbia Univ. Press, 1921.

Garraghan, Gilbert J. A Guide to Historical Method. N. Y.: Fordham Univ. Press, 1946.

Gottschalk, Louis. Understanding History; a Primer of Historical Method. N. Y.: Knopf, 1950.

Hulme, Edward II. History and its Neighbors. London, Oxford Univ. Press, 1942.

Johnson, Allen. The Historian and Historical Evidence. N. Y.: Scribner, 1934.

Kent, Sherman. Writing History. N. Y.: Crofts, 1946.

Langlois, C. V., and Seignobes, C. Introduction to the Study of History. Translated by G. G. Berry. N. Y.: Holt, 1903.

Nevins, Allan. The Gateway to History. Boston: Heath, 1938. Especially Chap. VII, "Pilate on Evidence."

Piper, Raymond F., and Ward, Paul L. The Fields and Methods of Knowledge. N. Y.: Crofts, 1939. Chap. IV. "History."

Robinson, James Harvey. The New History. N. Y.: Macmillan, 1927.

Shera, J. H. "The Literature of American Library History." Library Quarterly, XV (1945). 1-24.

_____. "On the Value of Library History." Library Quarterly, XXII (1952) pp. 240-251.

Shotwell, James T. The History of History. N. Y.: Columbia Univ. Press, 1929.

Social Science Research Council. Committee on Historiography. Theory and Practice in Historical Study. N. Y.: Soc. Sci. Research Council, n. d. (Bulletin no. 54) Especially Chap. II. Randall, John H. and Haines, George. "Controlling Assumptions in the Practice of American Historians."

Vincent, John M. Historical Research; an Outline of Theory and Practice. N. Y.: Holt, 1911.

CHAPTER III

HISTORY OF HISTORICAL WRITING

Greek Historiography

Before the age of the Greek historians and the development of
historical writing in the modern sense, such conscious historical record as has survived may be categorized into two major classes --
theocratic history and myth. The former, of which the writings of
the Old Testament are an excellent example, was a narration of e-
vents demonstrating the influence of a god, or gods, conceived in the
form of a super-human sovereign, directing the actions of men. The
purpose of such writing was not conscious historical record, but to
make known to the worshippers of the deity in question the deeds
whereby his power was made manifest. Myth, as distinct from theocratic history, deals exclusively with super-human beings, is not concerned with human action, and conceives the events narrated as having taken place in a "dateless" past. Theocratic history may, and often does, recount events which are verifiable by the use of modern
historical evidence, though its interpretation of causality differs considerably from that of the modern historian. Myth, on the other hand,
is pure invention, though it may have had its origin in some actual occurrence or observed phenomenon for which an explanation is sought--
the Creation, the assumed course of the sun about the earth, the cause
of lightning and thunder, the sequence of the seasons, the mystery of
birth and death. Such was the course of historical writing, or rather
of quasi-historical writing, in the Near East from the Mediterranean
to Mesopotamia, and in Egypt and the other Northern African coast-
lands, until Herodotus and Thucydides gave to history its modern point
of view.

This theocratic and mythical history was not alien to the Greek
mind. The poems of Homer are legend and to a very great extent
they are theocratic, and even in the writings of the fifth-century historians these elements are not absent, for they are to be found in both
Herodotus and Thucydides. But the Hellenic influence gave to history,
for the first time, a true scholarship, and a recognition that its main
concern was with human, not theistic, actions. On the other hand,
Greek thought was, in a sense, antithetical to the growth of historical
scholarship or at least inhospitable to the growth of historical thought.
To the Greeks science was a search for eternal verities -- for the
straight line and the plane surface as the mathematician thinks of
them -- objects which cannot change their characteristics. History,
on the other hand, must perforce deal with change, with that which is
transitory and impermanent and must accept evidence based only upon
momentary sensuous perception. Such a study, therefore, could not

be a science or the basis of a science.

This does not mean that the Greeks were hostile to history. Living in a time when events were moving with extraordinary rapidity, they were intensely conscious of change. Thus knowing that life cannot go on unchanged, they were particularly eager to discover what those changes had been that had brought the present into existence, and how a knowledge of the changes of the past could better equip the present to make prognostic judgments. If the course of history was flexible and modifiable the study of history would then have a utilitarian purpose, for it could teach the individual how to shape the future for the benefit of himself and of society.

The great contribution of Herodotus was that in this intellectual climate of legend and of myth he was the first to bring forth a true scholarship of history. He recognized that the historian must begin with the asking of questions, an awareness of his own ignorance, a belief that history is concerned with human behavior, and that it exists for human self-knowledge. Yet he did not understand the problem of historical causation as we conceive of it today, but wrote history to the end that the deeds of his predecessors might not be forgotten.

The major strength, and at the same time the most important limitation, of the historical writing of both Herodotus and Thucydides was that it drew almost exclusively for its sources upon the accounts of eyewitnesses. The ability to cross-examine a living witness in the best Socratic method gave to historical inquiry a solid foundation of scholarship, and one might even go so far as to say that the Greek historians of the fifth century in their methods of investigation anticipated the modern interview technique of the sociologists. This ability of the historian to wring from his informant the information he sought, to confront one witness with the account of another, and to take full advantage of the interplay of mind on mind, gave to the historian a confidence and solidity denied to those dependent upon only recorded information. But the method imposed upon its users an attenuated historical perspective, a perspective that was no greater than the length of living memory. Further, it limited the historian in the choice of his subject to that which had taken place within the memories of those with whom he could have personal contact. Very literally, then, the Greek historian did not choose his subject, his subject chose him. This does not mean that Herodotus and Thucydides did not make use of information beyond the memories of their contemporaries, but when they did, myth and legend were introduced into their historical narratives and their work was correspondingly less reliable. The essential fact is not that the remote past was for the Greek historians beyond the scope of their scholarship, but that the recent past was well within their grasp. They had invented historical scholarship and though its field was still narrow, within its limits it was secure.

Thucydides was not an intellectual descendant of the Herodotean tradition for Herodotus had no successors. Rather, the dominant influence upon Thucydides, as C. N. Cochrane has pointed out[1], was that of Hippocratic medicine, which gave to historical scholarship a psychological emphasis and a desire to discover in the events of history, or a complex of those events, laws or principles which demonstrate the existence of universal verities. Thucydides believed that history does repeat itself and that future generation can learn from past events in such a way that history itself can become a guide to action in the present. Whereas Herodotus was primarily concerned with the events of history themselves, Thucydides was interested in differentiating between the real and the apparent motives that impelled action. Thus his historical reconstruction is heavily weighted with commentary upon motives and inventions, and the speeches which he put into the mouths of his historical characters were an attempt, not to reconstruct what they actually said, but what they should have said under the circumstances within which they were operating. Whether or not this is the proper function of the historian, Thucydides was the first to analyze historical causality in such psychological terms.

Though one may not so regard them today, both Herodotus and Thucydides were writers of "popular" history. Their narratives were not prepared for a limited academic circle but for the general reading public. Herodotus sought to reveal the truth about the past for the understanding of his fellow men. Thucydides searched history for evidences of universal truths concerning the nature of man in society. Neither was consciously writing for the delectation of some future pedagogue or to give some nineteenth century schoolboy practice in reading Greek. The line of demarcation between scholarship and "popularization" is seldom sharp, and the "popular" work of one age may well be the "scholarship" of the next.

As the Greek world expanded through the conquests of Alexander the Great and as the Barbarians assumed the elements of Greek culture through the process of Hellenization, there arose a new group of historians who could feel themselves imaginatively as contemporaries of Herodotus and Thucydides and yet remain of their own century, able to compare their times with the past. This new world-history could not be written from the testimony of living eye-witnesses, but was compiled from the writings of those "authorities" who set down accounts of particular societies or events at particular periods.

Roman Historiography

This new "scissors-and-paste" history was inherited by the Romans from the Hellenistic period, and attained full growth in the work of Polybius, who was himself a Greek. Unlike the Greeks, the Romans were acutely conscious of their historical continuity with the past, and

---

[1]
C. N. Cochrane. Thucydides and the Science of History. (London, 1929). 180 pp.

preserved, to an extent unknown to the Greeks, the ancient traditions of their own corporate history. Though Polybius came to Rome during the golden age of the Republic as an enemy, he remained to praise its civilization. "The Greeks," he wrote, " are nothing but incorrigible children compared to the Romans." His primary objective was to narrate the conquest of the world by Rome as the natural consequence of the superiority of her civilization. While his history begins with a Rome that is mature and fully formed, ready to initiate her conquests, he at least opens his story more than a century and a half before the time of composition. Only at that point, in his opinion, do the authorities become reliable, so that he does not attempt to discover how a national spirit comes into existence. Doubtless he was familiar with the traditions concerning the origins of the Roman people, but he regarded such myths as beyond the limits of historical scholarship, and not trustworthy as reliable evidence.

Polybius thought of himself as the first to conceive of history as a special discipline having a universal value. Thus he ascribes to the study of history the pragmatic and utilitarian virtue of developing in the individual statesman the ability and self-discipline essential to the successful conduct of political life. By this he does not mean that it teaches one generation of leaders to avoid the mistakes of its predecessors. Rather, it leads not to a victory over circumstance but to a mastery of self. The influence of fortune bulks large in his concept of history, but what one learns from the tragedies of its heroes is not to circumvent misfortune but to develop fortitude in the face of adversity.

With Livy the goal of a complete history of Rome was achieved. His whole task was to assemble all the available traditional records cf early Roman history and weld them into a single continuous narrative. To the Roman mind, which thought of Roman history as the only history worth preserving, this meant the writing of "universal" history on a truly "grand" scale.

Livy made no pretense to originality either as to materials or method, but based his claim to preeminence upon his literary style, which is outstanding. Further, he wrote with high moral purpose -- to present the remote past so that contemporary Rome might learn that its greatness had its foundations in a primitive morality that dated from a time when Roman society was simple and uncorrupted. His attempts to preserve a critical attitude toward his sources were sincere. Confronted by a mass of legends he neither rejected them nor repeated them as being substantially accurate, but he presented them with caution, warning that they show a tendency to magnify fact and to intermingle divine intervention with human action. He did not search out the origins of tradition nor did he attempt to discover the various distorting media through which they had passed.

The followers of Livy did not try to improve upon his work, but either copied him or confined their writings to the immediate past, and so far as method is concerned Tacitus represented a decline. Tacitus is generally conceded to be the greatest name in Roman historiography, though one might question whether he was really a historian at all. Certainly he was less interested in ascertaining the facts and presenting the truth as he discovered it than in indicting the emperors and with them, by implication, the government itself. To establish his point of view, he employed sources drawn from the literature of detraction which was surreptitiously circulated during every reign and would have achieved no permanence had it not been for the borrowings of Tacitus. As a historian, then, Tacitus must be read with great caution. Not only was his work distorted by bias, but he systematically represented history as essentially the clash of characters in which exaggerated virtue and vice were in perpetual conflict. Thus, though he has been praised for his character presentation, those characters are never clearly understood or analyzed, but are in effect the incarnation of virtue or evil, delineated without insight or sympathy.

But one cannot dismiss the barren wastes of Roman historiography without at least mention of one writer who is less a historian than a moralist, but is significant because of the influence which his writings have exerted upon English letters. The Graeco-Roman mind was more interested in biography than in narrative history, not only because biography could be made the vehicle of moralizing and other forms of didactic historical writing but also for the reason that the lives of the leaders of a nation or people were closely associated with the fortunes of the state. This vogue for biography reached its height in Plutarch's Parallel Lives, wherein the biography of a Roman is compared with that of a Greek to prove the moral superiority of the latter. For though Plutarch admired the civilization and the political solidity of Rome, he did not forsake his native Greece, in whose leaders he found a sensitivity to moral influences to which the Romans were largely indifferent. Like his predecessors Plutarch wrote history for a didactic purpose, a passionate zeal to recreate for his contemporaries the long-vanished Greek idealism and reverence for morality. Plutarch's writings do not represent our modern concept of the ancients, but from the Renaissance to the French Revolution he enjoyed a tremendous popularity. The intense individualism of the Renaissance and the rebirth of interest in the Classical world revived his work from the neglect it had suffered during the Middle Ages. Shakespeare's concept of Graeco-Roman history is almost entirely shaped by Plutarch as seen through North's translation. Dryden's translation again revived his popularity among eighteenth century English scholars, and the spirit of the French Revolution with its admiration for the Classical world as contrasted with the demoralization of the Ancien Regime brought Plutarch an even wider audience. Though he made no contribution to historical scholarship, and his portraits must be regarded with the utmost skepticism, he may still be read with pleasure by those who seek refuge in ideas and ideals from the materialism of modern civilization.

The great contribution of Graeco-Roman historiography was that it represented a turning from theocratic history and myth to an inquiry into the true nature of actual events and the actions of man. Though it did not entirely reject the influence of the divine and the supernatural it attempted to develop a real scholarship in historical writing. Its great weakness lay in its emphasis on the didactic and what Collingwood calls "substantialism" -- the search for eternal verities that were thought to underly the continuing process of historical change.

The character of historical writing in the Classical world clearly reflects the status of libraries at that time. Herodotus and Thucydides, depending as they did upon the accounts of eye-witnesses and the memories of their contemporaries, had relatively little need for extensive library resources, and indeed there were few materials available to them. There seems sufficient evidence to indicate that by the end of the fifth century B. C. books were fairly plentiful in Greece, though an extensive reading public was not developed until the time of Aristotle, who himself assembled one of the largest and most important private libraries of the Classical world.

With the advent of "synthetic" or scissors-and-paste-history, inherited by the Romans from the Greeks, the need for extensive library resources was obviously imperative, and by that time there had developed many public and private collections in both Greece and Rome. The reputation of the libraries of Alexandria, Pergamum, and Athens is so extensive that one is likely to forget that remains of many small local libraries have been found in ancient Greece. Rome characteristically absorbed the bibliographical resources of Greece and Egypt. and added collections of her own making. The Roman empire, by conquering a vast number of independent city-states in which organic political life was locally focussed, also assimilated great quantities of archival materials that were invaluable to the historian. Further, the golden age of Latin literature from the first century B. C. to the first century A. D. was characterized by the collection of many private libraries assembled mainly by the wealthy classes and kept in their palaces and villas, where they could be consulted by scholars and others who might have need for them. Lacking such resources the work of Polybius, Livy, and Tacitus and their contemporaries would have been impossible. [2]

Medieval Historiography

Classical historiography disappeared in the fifth century, and for eight hundred years thereafter the writing of history was domin-

---

[2]
For discussions of ancient libraries in the Classical World see:
Alfred Hessel. A History of Libraries. Trans. by Reuben Peiss. (Washington, D. C.: Scarecrow Press, 1950), Chap. I.
Edward A. Parsons. The Alexandrian Library. (N. Y.: Elsevier Press, 1953), 468 pp.
James Westfall Thompson. Ancient Libraries. (Berkeley: Univ. of California Press, 1940), 120 pp.

ated by churchmen. So complete was the domination that the contribution of laymen to history was practically non-existent until the thirteenth century.

The spread of Christianity brought to historical writing a new orientation, purpose, and concept of causality. For the Hellenic metaphysical faith in the existence of eternal verities, Christianity substituted but one eternal verity -- God. Since everything had been created by God, all things, including people, nations, and the course of history were His work. They were not eternal, but could be altered, reoriented, abolished to comply with His divine plan. It was not given to man always to know God's will; hence, arose a kind of blindness in human action, a necessity that impelled one to act without knowing what the results of that action might be.

The impact upon historical writing of this belief in a theocentric universe could not but be profound. Fundamentally it gave to history a new importance, for to the church the historical process became a demonstration of the development of God's plan. History then was regarded as one of the best sources for the evidence of Divine power, and the actions of men assumed an importance not in and for themselves but as vehicles of Divine will. Thus the process of historical change was not fortuitous but the very essence of historical substance. Finally, Christianity gave to mankind a new awareness of the unity of history, for if all peoples and all nations are essential to the development of God's plan, and if the historical process is everywhere and always operating, every part of history is a unit of the whole.

This complete reorientation of historical thought gave to historical writing during the early Christian period certain marked characteristics. Basically it became a universal history that began with the creation of the world, for the past, whether pagan or Christian, was a manifestation of God's plan. In consequence there appeared great numbers of world chronicles, universal histories, and monastic annals. Secondly, events were not the results of human wisdom or ignorance, but segments in a pre-ordained course. Thus history not only assumed a pattern but the focus of history became the life of Christ. The past was in effect dichotomized into the pre-Christian and the Christian eras; an age of darkness and an age of light. This division of the historical continuum into two major portions led to further division into epochs, periods, or ages, each with its own peculiar characteristics, and each distinguished by some central event, less important than the birth of Christ but significant in its own way, which gave to each epoch some attribute or set of attributes that distinguished it from all others. Thus was given to history a single chronological framework that dated everything with reference to the birth of Christ. Such a concept of history resulted in the Chronographia of Eusebius, which terminated in 324 but was continued to 379 by St. Jerome, and from which sprang a whole family of chronicles including such significant works as those of Cassiodorus in Italy during the sixth century, Isider of Seville a

century later, and in England the monumental work of the Venerable
Bede, who died in 735. This concept of the epoch-making event, and
with it the idea of the division of history into periods, each with its
own peculiar character soon became a tradition in historical writing
that has persisted even to the present day.

The medieval historian was largely dependent for his facts upon
tradition, to the interpretation of which he brought no critical machinery other than a naive credulity, though his work is often buttressed
with great stylistic merit and imaginative power. His great task was
not to praise a nation, a people, or an individual, but to discover and
expound the objectives of the Divine Plan. Unlike the true historian who
restricts himself to the past, and who makes no pretense to a knowledge
of the future, the medieval scholar wrote history that looked forward
to the end of history as that which is foreordained by God and made
known to man through revelation. History, thus, became in a sense
the hand-maiden of eschatology, since the ultimate goal of history was
the consummation of the Divine Plan. From the abstract and philosophical humanism of Graeco-Roman historiography the medieval historian
turned to an equally abstract theocentric view of mankind, and seeking
the essence of history outside history itself, turned away from the actions of men to the revelation of God.

That the Church preserved the cultural heritage of the Western
World through a thousand years of intellectual darkness and barbarism
is denied only by those who are uncompromisingly opposed to the Church
itself. The part played by the monastic libraries in Ireland, England,
and on the Continent in the preservation of that culture has been often
narrated. The writing of universal history within the frame of reference established by the Church made demands upon the book resources
of an age in which books were far from plentiful. The churchmen ransacked such collections as those of the library at Caesarea, which was
known to have been extensively used by Eusebius, the monasteries of
St. Gall, Reichenau, Cluny, Iona and her dependent houses (in which
were assembled some of the finest collections of Ireland) and St.
Albans, to which Archbishop Aelfric bequeathed his personal collection
of books. Throughout the western world monks were set to the task of
copying manuscripts, not only because it provided an opportunity for
men who might otherwise suffer from indolence, but because the books
were needed. Typically the medieval manuscript displayed crude and
careless workmanship, but such rare jewels as the books of Kells and
Armagh are eloquent testimony to the standards of artistry that could
be attained in an age which is characteristically thought of as averse to
the beautiful. [3]

3
  Richard de Bury. Philobiblion. (Berkeley: Univ. of California
Press, 1948), 110 pp.
  George Haven Putnam. Books and Their Makers During the
Middle Ages. (N. Y.: Putnam, 1897-98), 2 v.
  James Westfall Thompson. The Medieval Library. (Chicago:
Univ. of Chicago Press, 1939), 682 pp.

Although the mediaeval historian had access to only the most meager sources, and to no bibliographic guides to locate those materials
that did exist, the period has been of lasting interest to later historians.
A good modern guide to both contemporary and later literature has been
prepared under the auspices of the Mediaeval Academy of America:

Paetow, Louis John. A Guide to the Study of Medieval History.
Rev. ed. New York: F. S. Crofts and Company, 1931. 643 pp.

Renaissance Historiography

The Renaissance, with its return to the classical learning of Greece
and Rome, brought with it a fresh reorientation of historical studies.
Once again history became homocentric, and man's actions were no
longer dwarfed into insignificance by divine direction. But man for the
Renaissance historian was not the individual presented by the ancient
writers, a being whose actions and destiny were the work of his own intellect. Rather, he bore the impression of the preceding centuries of
Christian indoctrination and became a creature of passion and of faith,
rather than of reason. History thus became an account of human passions as a manifestation of human nature.

So began a complete re-examination of history in which earlier
myths and misconceptions were rejected and disproved -- a new desire to reconstruct the past with as much accuracy as limited records
could provide. By the seventeenth century, when Sir Francis Bacon
divided all knowledge into the tri-partite classification of the faculties
-- Memory, Reason, and Imagination -- he was tacitly acknowledging
that the primary responsibility of history was to recall and record the
past with the greatest possible fidelity. Here was a denial of the Medieval faith that the historian could foretell the future, or that history's
main objective was to discover the Divine Plan that constitutes the
framework for historic facts. The discovery of the facts themselves,
for their own sake, was the task of the historian. Bacon never inquired
into the manner in which the historian would supplement the deficiencies
and limitations of memory; at least, the historian had a program of action, even though he lacked the critical apparatus through which such a
program could be put into effect.

Livy, and later Polybius, who was so admired by Machiavelli, supplied the classical patterns for the historians of the Italian renaissance.
Leonardo Bruni was the first to strip the history of Florence from the
tangle of legend attached to it. Polydore Vergil, who flouted the tales
of Geoffrey of Monmouth and the legends of King Arthur, was the first
to lay a solid foundation for the study of English history. The popularity of biography for the Renaissance reader is evident from the success of such works as Boccaccio's Life of Dante and Benvenuto Cellini's
history of himself.

This renewed search for historical facts and the revival of interest in antiquity was also expressed in the discovery of archaeology as

34

an aid to historical scholarship. In the fourteenth century for the first time, the value of inscriptions, coins, medals, and other artifacts, became apparent to the historian, and by 1460 collections of antiquities in Rome and Florence had been assembled.

Germany, on the eve of the Reformation, evinced a rapid intellectual growth. Such universities as Freiburg, Basel, Tübingen, Mainz, and Wittenberg were founded, important libraries were assembled, and the classics were translated. This revival of classical studies stimulated an interest in antiquity, and the thought of the German humanists was distinctly historical in its orientation. But the struggles that characterized the Reformation and Counter-Reformation arrested and finally destroyed this humanistic interest, and once again history became the hand-maiden of theologic dogma.

In England the Tudor period, which began in 1485 and ended with the death of Elizabeth in 1603, received from the Renaissance a great expansion of man's mental horizons. This was further extended by widened commercial contacts and an increased knowledge of geography and cosmology. Every such extension led to the production of written records or discussions, many of which are the roots of the separate academic disciplines or subject fields of today. Explorers proved the existence of new lands and new peoples, and through the advances of physical science man's concept of the universe was completely revolutionized. The age produced a few names of limited importance in the field of historiography -- Polydore Vergil, Sir Thomas More, George Cavendish -- but in general it was in pure literature that the period made its greatest contribution. By the close of the fifteenth century the medieval monastic chronicle had been supplanted by the city chronicle written in English by lay authors, but formal narrative history was vastly overshadowed by the accumulation of documentary sources; state papers, letters, parliamentary proceedings, accounts of foreign envoys, and records of state trials. The concept of formal history during the Elizabethan age was extremely limited. It lacked historical perspective and gave little weight to the relative importance of the events it narrated. It drew heavily and uncritically from such sources as Holinshed's Chronicles, and much of it was written to glorify an expanding English nationalism and the achievements of Elizabeth.

The movement for the establishment of library collections begun by the monastic orders during the Middle Ages increased at a greatly accelerated pace during the Renaissance and the decades that followed. Three factors contributed to this expanded rate of growth. The revival of interest in antiquity characteristic of this period brought with it a correlative demand for books. The establishment of universities in England and on the Continent made the assembly of books for the use of scholars mandatory. Finally, the invention of printing with movable type and the spread of this innovation throughout the western world greatly increased the availability of the recorded word and thus made the public and private accumulation of books possible on a scale previously unattainable. Even as early as the latter half of the fifteenth century, town libraries were established in Germany, at Frankfort,

and Mainz, to be followed shortly thereafter by Stadt-Bibliotheken at
Hanover and Magdeburg. Private collections were growing in magnitude and significance and many of these found their way into the libraries of towns and universities. Library promotion thus was no longer
the special province of the Church, but became an activity in which the
entire scholarly world had a deep concern. To attempt here a catalogue
of the libraries formed during this period would be irrelevant, but the
chronological tables which conclude John Thornton's Chronology of
Librarianship[4] are eloquent testimony of the magnitude of this movement.

Reference has already been made to the proliferation of documents
during this period, and though the great era of archival expansion was
still to come, there was, nevertheless, at this time a genuine concern for the preservation of official records. The growing complexities of government, as national states emerged from the feudal regime,
and the expansion of international commerce and trade, as well as historical consciousness, contributed to the urge to preserve archival
materials. The great national archives had not yet come into existence, but numerous small local collections were assembled throughout
England, Germany, France, and other European countries -- already
the foundations of modern archival practice were being laid.

During the manuscript age, copies of works were so rare that it
was a matter of great importance for scholars to know where a copy
of a given title might be located. As a rule this information was passed
from person to person and became part of the lore of scholarship.
Around 1410, John Boston of Bury began to compile the first union catalogue, a list of all the books in the various monasteries and other ecclesiastical houses of England which were known to him. To each library he assigned a number and after each title on the list, which was
arranged alphabetically by author, he placed the numbers indicating
location. This anticipates our modern union list by five centuries.

But perhaps of even greater significance was the publication in
1494 of Johann Tritheim's Liber de Scriptoribus Ecclesiasticis, a chronological listing of the writings, mainly but not exclusively ecclesiastical, of nearly one thousand authors. The compilation encompassed
some seven thousand titles, and gave ample evidence of genuine bibliographical research on the part of its editor. A year later he published
at Mainz his Catalogus Illustrium Virorum Germaniae, in which are
chronologically enumerated over two thousand works by more than three
hundred authors. With these two important works systematic bibliography may truly be said to have begun. One-half century later (1545)
Konrad Gesner published his Bibliotheca Universalis and rightfully
earned the title of the "father of universal bibliography." In this folio

---

4
John L. Thornton. Chronology of Librarianship. (London:
Grafton, 1941), pp. 157-166.
See also Hessel. op. cit. Chap. 5.

36

of thirteen hundred pages are listed, with annotation, approximately twelve thousand titles - all the Latin, Greek, and Hebrew books known to Gesner. The arrangement was alphabetical by the Christian names of the authors, but the work was followed three years later by the Pandectarum sive Partitionum Universalium, in which the titles of the preceding work were rearranged according to subject classes, only nineteen of which appeared, medicine and theology being omitted. Gesner had not only made a monumental contribution to universal bibliography, but he had set forth one of the first examples of bibliographic classification. These were not the only bibliographical undertakings of Tritheim and Gesner, nor were they alone concerned with such labor. In addition to these attempts to compile universal bibliography, there was a great proliferation of catalogues of particular library collections. The significant fact is that by the end of the sixteenth century the bulk of recorded literature was already so great that scholars felt the need for some systematization of it. Modern problems of bibliographic organization are at least as old as the printed book itself, and have become intensified with each change in the volume and nature of publication. [5]

Descartes and the Age of Reason

The spirit of the seventeenth and eighteenth centuries was, in many ways, as antithetical to history as had been that of the golden age of Greek philosophy. The age of reason concentrated its thought upon the problems of natural science and in large measure pushed history aside. Galileo and Newton had revolutionized rational thought. Mathematics was elevated to the highest position among sciences, and exactness and demonstrability became the supreme criteria of all scholarship. This was the age of the rapid rise of the scientific academies and societies.

Against the work of the historian, Descartes in his Discourse on Method brought to bear four major criticisms: (a) The historian is essentially a traveller in a foreign land, and like anyone who remains away from home too long, he becomes an alien to his own age. (b) Historical narratives cannot be trustworthy accounts of the past because of the nature of the record available to the historian. (c) Such untrustworthy history can have no value for the present as an aid to the solution of contemporary problems. (d) History is fantasy, and the picture of the past which it presents is more splendid than it actually was.

5

Theodore Besterman. The Beginnings of Systematic Bibliography. (Oxford: Oxford Univ. Press, 1935), 81 pp.

Descartes' contempt for history did not discourage the historians, who set about the application of Cartesian principles to historical method. They argued that if the natural world was mechanically constituted and general laws could be applied to nature, then it necessarily followed that man, as a product of nature, was also ruled by "natural laws" and his conduct could be interpreted in terms of axiomatic formulation as precise as those of Euclidean geometry. Cartesian historiography was rooted in a faith in reason and the dogma of infallible laws that in the eighteenth century grew to resemble the thirteenth century devotion to Divine ordination.

Though the spirit of the Age of Reason and of the Enlightenment was not disposed to view history with sympathy, the rationalistic school of historians did introduce new methods of historical criticism and did enlarge the content of history to include such auxiliary sciences as geography, geology, and climatology, each with its own specialized literature. Historians became aware of the influence of the physical environment upon the actions of men. Science had opened strange new vistas into the past of the human race, and historians began to ask: How old is man? Is modern society rooted in savagery? What was the nature of primitive society? How did the various forms of government originate and develop, and what is the best form? Finally, what is the real meaning of the human adventure? Montesquieu, who sought to establish a real science of society, explained the origin and development of political institutions and the laws of government. Because he began with the assumption that social phenomena, like physical phenomena, were subject to general laws, his analytical method served to bring to a subject that had previously been badly confused, a much needed order and clarity. Voltaire ridiculed the theocentric concept of history and derided the collection of human opinions concerning past events as little more than a recording of human errors. His credo as he set it forth in the article on History in Diderot's Encyclopedie held that history should concern itself with the search for more precise information, and a greater interest in customs, laws, mores, commerce, art, science, amusements, manner, and all the activities of daily life. Finally, this scientific orientation of historical scholarship renewed awareness of the historical importance of coins, inscriptions, seals, and non-literary documents and of their value as checks against the literary history that had been written by previous generations. The scope of history, as Voltaire pointed out, like that of mathematics and physics, had increased tremendously through the impact of the Cartesian method.

Gibbon, however, could find no better single principle or law about which to orient his history than human irrationality. In spite of the magnificence of his canvas, the massiveness of his historical structure, and the scholarly accuracy of much of his work, especially in the early volumes of the Decline and Fall, his historical narrative seems to find its focus in the triumph of barbarism over religion, and much of it is "little more than the register of the crimes, follies, and misfortunes of mankind."

Though the Age of Reason may have made important contributions to the methodology of history it did not deepen its spirit. It brought to bear upon history no values except the quantitative values of an emerging science. Society, at best, was only an agglomeration of human beings mechanically disposed and regulated. No account had been taken of the imponderables by which men live -- feeling, imagination, idealism, fantasy. So sterile did the treatment of historical causality become that Pascal could remark that had Cleopatra's nose been longer the entire history of the world would have been changed. In despair of genuine explanation historians attributed to the most trivial of causes the most important of effects. Cartesian historiography perished of its own detrition before the eighteenth century ended in the turmoil and the holocaust of the French Revolution.

Anti-Cartesianism

The first to lead the attack against the rationalists was the brilliant Neapolitan historian Vico, who set about the formulation of historical principles as Bacon had developed the principles of science. He did not deny the validity of mathematical knowledge, but he did impugn the Cartesian theory that no other kind of knowledge was valid. To him, only that which the human mind has directly experienced or constructed is truly comprehensible by the human mind. Thus Nature is intelligible only to God, but mathematics is intelligible to man because it is the product of his own formulation. It necessarily follows, then, that history, which is obviously the product of human endeavor, is particularly significant as an aspect of human knowledge. He saw history as the discipline which deals with the genesis and development of human societies and their institutions, and the historical process as that by which human beings construct systems of language, customs, laws, and government.

From his investigations into the nature of primitive society and the development of language and law he came to believe that history is divisible into periods, each of which had a general character that was reflected in every detail of the life of that period and reappeared in modified form in other periods. Further, he anticipated the cyclical theorists of today, such as Sorokin, Spengler, and Toynbee. In general his cycles assumed the following sequence: (a) the barbaric period of brute strength; (b) the heroic age of valiant strength; (c) the period of valiant justice; (d) the epoch of brilliant originality and constructive reflection; and finally (e) a period of spendthrift and wasteful opulence that destroyed that which had taken so long to build. He was not blinded by this passion for the historic cycle, but admitted that it was subject to variation and exception, not rigid or fixed. Finally he believed that this cycle was manifest in the form of a spiral, for history never really repeated itself, but each period was altered and modified by that which had gone before.

To historians Vico issued a number of warnings against certain prejudices that he found prevalent in the work of his predecessors and contemporaries. Briefly stated these prejudices were: (a) The belief in the magnificence of antiquity that exaggerates the wealth, power, and grandeur of the civilization that the historian is studying; (b) The propensity of every historian to present the past of his own nation in more favorable terms than is justified by the facts; (c) The fallacy of the academic mind of the historian which leads him to present the historic figures about whom he is writing as being, like himself, scholars, students, or at least individuals of a reflective, intellectual type; (d) The error which leads the historian to believe that because two civilizations evince the same beliefs or institutions the one must have borrowed it from the other - a prejudice that denies the creative power of the human mind and its capacity to rediscover ideas for itself without learning them from previous society; and (e) The historian's assumption that the ancients knew more about their times than he because of the advantage of temporal propinquity when actually he might know much more about the origins of their own institutions than they themselves knew.

Positively, Vico indicated certain methods and disciplines available to the historian that would contribute to the validity of his results. He demonstrated that the study of language and etymology could contribute much to an understanding of the life of a people or civilization, and he used mythology to exemplify the social structure of a people whose myths he was investigating. Further, he proposed the use of tradition, not as a guide to literal truth, but as a confused group memory of facts, a refraction index that would reveal the social patterns of the ancients. Finally, he emphasized his belief that human minds at like stages of development tend to create similar institutions, social patterns, civilizations; a conviction which was basic to his cyclical concept of the historical continuum.

The thought of Vico was far in advance of his time, and his influence among those historians who were dominated by the Cartesian philosophy was slight. Not until the end of the eighteenth century, when he was discovered by the German scholars, was the magnitude of his contribution to historical method truly appreciated. Today sociologists and economists, as well as historians, acknowledge indebtedness to him.

A second attack against the Cartesians came from a group who were philosophers rather than historians but who developed a point of view that recognized history as a valid discipline and reoriented philosophy in the direction of history. This school of thought, of which the leaders were Locke, Berkeley, and Hume, denied the existence of innate ideas and insisted that all knowledge came through human experience. Historical investigation thus became the gateway through which man learned most about the origin and development of human knowledge and human error. From this group, the immediate influence of which was much greater than that of Vico, historiography achieved a rational, pragmatic, anti-metaphysical spirit, developed a basic concern for the problem of causation, and was lifted above the older chronicles of war and the genealogies of rulers to a level that made truly scientific approach to history possible.

Library Development During the Enlightenment

During the Age of Reason and the Enlightenment the movement for the establishment of libraries, begun by the monastic schools and augmented by the universities, grew at an increasingly rapid rate. As scholarship during the seventeenth and eighteenth centuries became more and more dependent upon the book, the demand for library collections, in both history and science, increased in intensity. The scholarship of this period was still largely the product of individual, and often isolated effort that was dominantly book-and library-centered. But in the seventeenth century scholars began to associate themselves into societies for the oral exchange of their accumulated knowledge and experience. The verbal transmission of information fostered by these early learned societies soon achieved a more permanent form when the publication of transactions and proceedings of such group deliberations was inaugurated.

The only means of scientific intercommunication available to the precursors of modern science was private correspondence, and many of the most important figures of that period maintained a voluminous and steady flow of personal letters. But the unreliability of such a form of communication is self-evident; it was far too dependent upon the fortuitous, the establishment of a friendly association rather than a hostile rivalry, or, at times, even upon geographical propinquity. The solution to such problems was clearly indicated when, in 1665, Denis de Sallo published the first volume of the Journal des scavans, which in its earlier years, was dominantly concerned with the work of the scientific societies. During this same year the Royal Society began its long and important series of Philosophical Transactions, and, as Miss Ornstein observes, "All subsequent scientific periodicals developed in imitation of these two."[6]

This was a book-centered scholarship which drew heavily from the past. Miss Ornstein estimates that in the publication of the first year of the Journal des scavans, "possibly one third of the articles are on historical researches."[7] Even in the field of the pure and applied sciences the historical approach was important, and in those few instances where elementary laboratory investigations were employed their techniques were derived from, and their results were carefully checked against, the published history of previous inquiries. The work of the

---

6
  Martha Ornstein. The Role of the Scientific Societies in the Seventeenth Century. (Chicago: Univ. of Chicago Press, 1938). 308 pp.
7
  Ibid. p. 201.

41

many scientific societies that were founded during this period was then oriented about library collections and implemented by the publication of scholarly journals.

Other groups of individuals banded together to procure collections of books that would satisfy their scholarly demands. This was the age of the inception of the social libraries, book clubs, and other forms of voluntary association that have as their objective the assembly of book collections for which the members felt a genuine need. In addition to those movements for the establishment of incipient popular libraries, which in the nineteenth century were to emerge as our modern public library system, there were founded during this period such great collections as those of the British Museum, the National Library of Turin, the National Library of Naples, the Moscow University Library, the National Library of Milan, the Royal Library at Stuttgart, the library of the National Institute of France, the National Library of Palermo, and on this side of the Atlantic the libraries of Harvard, Yale, Columbia and Princeton, and the collections of the Massachusetts Historical Society.

The increased interest in historical documents was reflected in the development of modern archival practice, especially in France and Germany. France, under the impact of the Revolution and the growth of bureaucracy, was the first European country to develop an archival system closely integrated with governmental administration. This French system strongly influenced other European countries, even though the French enthusiasm for centralization and regulation was not always slavishly followed. By 1770 there were some five thousand archives in all of France, of which four hundred were in Paris alone. In 1789 the Revolution threw open the archives of the Ancien Regime, the private records of the feudal lords, and the clergy as well as those of the Royal house. This vast body of material then became the property of the state and the task that confronted the new government was to organize it and to bring it under control. To this end the Archives Nationales were established and the country embarked on the long undertaking of coordinating the archival processes of national and local governments. The problem was simplified by the destruction of great quantities of material through the misdirected zeal of the Revolutionists. Estimates of this destruction run as high as five hundred million pieces, but despite this wanton prodigality, the preservation of government records as a proper concern of the state had become an acknowledged principle, and our modern system of national archival practice had begun.

The emergence of interest in science brought with it the desire to formulate principles and to devise schemes of classification, not only for the phenomena of man's environment, but for books and the contents of libraries as well. Modern bibliothecal classification derived from scientific classification. Little is known about the origins of library classification, but the assumption seems valid that early libraries were generally arranged by size and volume or in broad categories arranged with but slight reference to logic. Monastic libraries customarily arranged their materials according to relationship to the Scriptures and

42

the Church service. But when Sir Francis Bacon devised his tripartite division of knowledge into Memory (History), Imagination (Poetry), and Reason (Science and Philosophy) he gave to library classification a basic pattern that has persisted, through the influence of Melvil Dewey and the Universal Decimal scheme, to the present day. Further, Bacon's scheme (which was, of course, not intended as a system for the arrangement of library materials), as modified by Diderot and d'Alembert, provided the framework for Thomas Jefferson's library classification. Jefferson's classification was adopted by the Library of Congress, when it acquired his library, and remained the basic plan for its book arrangement until the turn of the twentieth century, when the present classification schedules were devised.

At about the time Bacon was deriving his classification from the three human faculties, the distinguished librarian of the Mazarin Library, Gabriel Naudé, developed a library classification in twelve major categories. [8] This and the system of the Paris Booksellers, modified by many hands, but especially by Brunet, were most influential on the Continent. Thus the growth of library collections to the point at which some system of arrangement became essential and the emergence of science with the desire to classify all phenomena converged to produce, in the seventeenth and eighteenth centuries, the formulation of principles of library classification to which modern librarianship is still heavily indebted.

The Beginnings of Scientific History

The tumultuous spirit of Romanticism, which gave to literature some of the best writing -- and some of the worst -- in spite of its excesses and lack of discipline, did contribute to historical writing an awareness that early civilizations had values of their own, values which had since been lost. To be sure, Romanticism produced the antiquarian and pseudo-Gothic trappings of a Strawberry Hill and the terror romances of Ann Radcliffe, but it also brought Bishop Percy's Reliques, a collection of English ballad literature. Even Rousseau's fanatical belief in the nobility of the savage fostered a sympathetic understanding of the past; a realization that history is sequential; a development of human reason in which the past stages of history led necessarily to the present. Thus the reconstruction of the Middle Ages became a recapitulation of the process which led to the present. The Romanticist did not minimize the gulf between the present and antiquity, but he bridged that chasm with an historical continuum that made of history a single process of development from a beginning in savagery to a cul-

---

8

Gabriel Naudé. Advice on Establishing a Library. (Berkeley: Univ. of California Press, 1950), 110 pp.

This important work is the first formal treatise on library organization and administration.

mination in civilized society. Here was a foundation, at least, upon
which the evolutionary theory of history could be built, and it stimulated the omnivorous and indiscriminate collecting of books, manuscripts, documents, and artifacts of antiquity that gave to future historians materials which otherwise might not have survived.

Johann Gottfried Herder, who died at the beginning of the nineteenth
century, anticipated by more than fifty years the development of the
Darwinian principle of evolution and its application to history. From
Kant and Rousseau he derived the genetic principle of historical unity and the belief in individualism. Though an evolutionist, he was
still under the influence of Rousseau and other Romanticists in his
failure to stress, as did the later evolutionists, the superiority of the
modern to the earlier stages of social development. His influence upon subsequent historians was very great; the Grimms' studies in folk-
lore, Karl Ritter's scientific geography, even Hegel and Von Ranke all
have Herderian antecedents. He was indeed the herald of the new historical scholarship, the "gate-keeper" of the nineteenth century.

The New History: Niebuhr and Ranke

Throughout the nineteenth century German scholarship dominated
historical writing; a leadership that began with the establishment in
1819 of the University of Berlin. To the faculty of that institution
Wilhelm von Humboldt brought such outstanding historians as Wolf,
Buttmann, Böckh, Heindorf, Spalding, Rhus, Niebuhr, and later
Hegel, Karl Otfried Müller, and Leopold von Ranke. The work of these
men made of the University a truly great international center for historical studies, the influence of which spread not only throughout
Europe but across the Atlantic to the United States where it became the
strongest single force in nineteenth century American historiography.
This new German scholarship was not content with mere erudition, but
sought to ascertain the significance and continuity of events, and thus
to perceive and understand the forces underlying history. With this,
came a scrupulous sifting of historical data, a relentless search for
accuracy in historical fact, an unceasing evaluation of source materials, and a publishing program that produced an imposing collection of
historical Monumenta. These benefits more than compensated for the
Prussian tendency to subordinate history to politics, especially Prussian
politics, which was evident even in the work of one as objective as Ranke.

In his History of Rome, Niebuhr's procedures were those of the exact scientist who weighs and evaluates every shred of evidence until
his conclusions, solidly supported by facts themselves, emerge. "I
dissect words," he wrote, "as the anatomist dissects bodies: I am
trying to separate from foreign matters a skeleton of fossil bones collected too carelessly." This was Roman history as it had never been
written before, and it inaugurated modern historiographic methods.
Though his practical experience as a statesman in the field of administration, finance, and diplomacy colored his point of view and deter-

mined his approach to history, he made important contributions to archaeology, philology, the restoration of palimpsests, and the editing and translating of significant documents. His methods largely set the pattern for nineteenth century historical scholarship both at home and abroad.

To the work of Niebuhr and his contemporaries Müller added the first comprehensive study of Greek culture, wherein he insisted that everything -- mythology, religion, politics, war, education, art -- was important to a balanced understanding of a society. Similarly, Savigny, in his investigations of historical jurisprudence in Germany brought to the study of law an awareness of the legal structure as an expression of the whole life of a people, and a realization that contemporary law was conditioned by the historical development of the legal process. Here again, this time in the field of codified law, one finds a pre-Darwinian exposition of continuity or evolution in social life. The scholars of the University of Berlin were bringing to fruition the growth for which, in the eighteenth century, Kant, Winckelmann, Wolf, and Herder had so ably prepared the soil.

Contemporary with these developments at Berlin, Arnold H. L. Heeren had well under way, at the University of Göttingen, his investigations into the history of commerce and colonization, and their effects upon the development of government and political institutions. Heeren's concern with the economic influences upon political history had begun with a schoolboy's interest in the revolt of the American Colonies against England, and later his thinking was profoundly shaped by the work of Adam Smith and Montesquieu. In his insistence upon the historical significance of the basic needs of men for food, clothing, and shelter, and the contribution of technological developments to the expansion of commerce and hence to the shaping of international politics, Heeren's point of view approaches that of the Marxian economic-determinists and the contemporary historians who emphasize the economic interpretation of history. To American historiography Heeren is of further importance because at Göttingen, under his direction, there studied during the early decades of the nineteenth century such American historians as Ticknor, Bancroft, and Motley. Also among his students was George Heinrich Pertz, whose scholarly editing of the Monumenta Germaniae Historica made it the greatest historical collection in the world, and the model for future scientific historical research through documentary analysis and criticism.

But among the many great German historians of the nineteenth century the towering figure is that of Leopold von Ranke, whose name has become synonymous with factual accuracy in historical research, and whose methods have been vigorously challenged and defended for more than half a century. His first book, Geschichte der romanischen and germanischen Volker, not only established his reputation as a historian of unusual promise, but it made three important contributions to contemporary historiography. It set forth the idea of the unity of the Romano-Germanic world, it exemplified a new standard of penetrating criticism of historical sources, and it declared for the first time the

45

author's determination to write history "wie es eigentlich gewesen ist." Von Ranke's determination to subject his sources to the most severe and uncompromising criticism and to reconstruct history as it actually happened led him to reject all previous general histories as virtually useless. The historian, if he is to avoid irresponsible interpretations, must make the fullest possible use of archival materials and other primary documents. Criticism, precision, penetration, these were the three rules which Von Ranke held ever before his students. The duty of the historian as he saw it was to minimize the subjective element which is inherent in every document. Obviously historians of the Von Rankean school would have much more use for archives than for libraries.

Von Ranke did not invent the seminar as an instrument for the training of historians, but he introduced it into the University of Berlin, and gave to it its widespread popularity. The objective of these seminars was twofold: to bring the student into a closer and more vital relationship with his teacher, and to train future teachers and research workers. His instruction was rarely theoretical, but consistently pragmatic; his methods those of a friendly, but severe, guide. From among his students there emerged more than a hundred eminent scholars who spread his influence throughout Germany, Europe, and the United States.

Within this limited space it is not possible even to list the writings which were the fruits of over sixty years of productive and indefatigable scholarship. Perhaps the best known were his History of the Popes, his history of France in the sixteenth and seventeenth centuries and of England in the seventeenth, and finally, his grand scheme to write a Weltgeschichte, of which seven volumes, to the reign of Otto the Great, A. D. 962, were published. For his work he ransacked the archives and libraries, both public and private, of Europe. His own private library of 25,000 volumes was piled chaotically on shelves and floor, for he objected to a classified arrangement because it would prevent him from finding what he wanted!

A thorough distrust of tradition, hearsay, and gossip, an intense hatred of mystery and speculation, an aversion to anything that was not recorded on paper and the accuracy of which could not be substantiated led him to neglect aspects of history for which no documentation existed. But his determination to present only the historic facts, however lacking in beauty they might be, led him to discover in the archives of Berlin, Vienna, Paris, Rome, Venice, and elsewhere, a great mass of important material which had been completely unknown.

One may justly charge that Von Ranke's insistence upon documentary proof narrowed the fields of his inquiry, caused him to reject much that was of value, and oriented his interpretation of history about a diplomatic and political center of gravity. One may also reasonably doubt that his objective, to write history as it actually happened, can ever be an attainable goal. But he was a profound scholar and a brilliant writer who shaped the course of historiography for generations. In 1884 when the American Historical Association was founded and

Von Ranke was elected its first and only honorary member. George Bancroft wrote to him, "We have meant this as a special homage to yourself as the greatest living historian." The Von Rankean school of historiography not only set the pattern of historical research to the eve of the first World War, but made history the dominant academic discipline of the nineteenth century.

In England the writing of history lagged seriously behind that in Germany and the remainder of the Continent. At the beginning of the nineteenth century, and for many decades thereafter, the writing of history in England was the handmaiden of belles-lettres, the occupation of amateurs, the vehicle for literary style. Macaulay, to whom facts were "but the dross of history," made the reading of history even more popular than had Sir Walter Scott, but he was intent upon the weaving of a literary tapestry, the presentation of a glowing reconstruction of the past. A strong Whig bias, a willingness to distort fact to fit his purpose, a fine disregard for accuracy, discredited him among fellow historians, but he was, without doubt, a great literary artist whose work has survived long after it was eclipsed by a more substantial but less brilliant historical scholarship.

In almost every way Carlyle was the antithesis of Macaulay. A pessimist who regarded conventional history as little more than glorified rumor, a moralist who saw in the historical continuum little more than the influence of heroic leadership, his French Revolution is a dramatic presentation of the interplay of human passions. His Oliver Cromwell and Frederick the Great are heroic portrayals of great men, presented, however, without a real understanding of the problems and forces that influenced their behavior and determined their policies.

Froude, the literary executor and biographer of Carlyle, was also a literary artist rather than a scientific historian, and, like Carlyle, primarily a moralist. Biased in his point of view and carelessly inaccurate, he was much criticized by his contemporaries for the deficiencies of his scholarship. But in extenuation one should point out that he did make extensive use of primary archival materials, worked diligently and painstakingly with almost illegible manuscripts, and gave to the figures of history a reality that made them something more human than saints or demons. Measured by the contemporary standards of German historical scholarship, his work is far from impressive, but he was not, as Edward Freeman charged, "the vilest brute that ever wrote a book."

The Influence of Nineteenth-Century Science

The impact of the Cartesian philosophy upon historical writing, and the foreshadowing of the doctrine of evolution in the work of Herder have already been pointed out. Nineteenth century science brought to historians a deepening sense of the importance of origin and structure, just as in the physical sciences scholars were intent upon discovering the basic structure of physical phenomena and organic unities. Thus

47

the aim of the Positivist school, under the influence of Comte's "Social Physics," sought to introduce into the study of society the same scientific observation and generalization that characterized chemistry, physics, and biology. Buckle in England and Taine in France became the outstanding exponents of the application of Comte's social doctrines to historical writing. The former rejected histories that were mere compilations of facts, and sought a true "science of history" through development of an inductive methodology. Taine, who was impressed by the importance of the milieu, saw history as a science analogous to physiology and zoology, rather than to mathematics and the exact sciences. Modern scholarship has rejected Taine's dogmatism and disparaged his accuracy, but it has adopted the central theme which all his work exemplifies, that history is concerned with the entire milieu -- the physical and social environment of a people -- and is not confined to the political life of the past.

The Darwinian theory of evolution gave to the historical continuum a new length, breadth, depth, and motivation. The historian became deeply indebted to the biologist for suggesting the organic nature of society. Bacteriology and medicine suggested that history could be written in terms of decay and decline as well as of progress and improvement. Even the Second Law of Thermo-Dynamics was adopted by a few historians to explain the rise and decay of civilization in terms of the exhaustion of energy.

Institutional, Social, and Economic History

The great emphasis, begun in Germany in the nineteenth century, upon the importance of archival and documentary sources led inevitably to the reconsideration of the history of institutions, particularly the origins of feudalism and the growth of cities and towns. Since archival materials are largely institutional in character and institutions are themselves not the products of theory but the result of a complex of social and economic forces their study, and the extensive archival investigations thus stimulated, were particularly fruitful and rewarding. The investigation of institutional history begun in Germany by Savigny, Paul Roth, and Waitz, was continued independently in France by the work of Guizot, Benjamin Guerard, and Fustel de Coulanges, who was especially noteworthy because of his mastery of documentary sources and his emphasis upon an objective analysis of such material. In England the movement was inaugurated in the middle of the century, by Hallam's Constitutional History of England, and Kemble's Saxons in England, but attained its fullest expression in the writings of Paul Vinogradoff, a Russian trained in the German seminars, and in Frederick William Maitland's constitutional history.

The writings in economic history present a vast area of scattered materials and contradictory theories, and its practitioners have never been certain whether they were economists or historians. There were historians with an economic point of view long before the development

48

in Germany of the economic school of historical writers. Aristotle, Plato, and in modern times, Bodin, Harrington, Voltaire, Heeren and Moser were all aware of the economic bases of society. In Germany the socio-economic school may be said to have begun with Roscher and Hildebrand, and includes such names as Knies, Schmoller, and especially Nitzsch and Lamprecht, though the latter was perhaps more of a sociologist and psychologist than a true historian. In England, where the industrial revolution made its greatest impact, and where the social organization was markedly different from that of nineteenth century Germany, the economic historians were less concerned with theories and generalizations concerning institutions and the state, and more absorbed in the individual and his relation to alterations in the economic system. Typical are J. E. Rogers' History of Agriculture and Prices in England in seven volumes, Cunningham's Growth of English Industry and Commerce, and, in the present century, Scott's Constitution and Finance of English, Scottish, and Irish Joint Stock Companies, and the work of George Unwin whose Industrial Organization, and Guilds and Companies of London, set forth his conviction that economic history supplies the best key to the problems of the growth of society.

Library Development During the Nineteenth Century

During the nineteenth century history, at long last, "came into its own," not only as a respectable discipline, but, together with the sciences, to a position of academic recognition. That the tremendous growth in the popularity of history, during these years, greatly encouraged the development and expansion of libraries and archives is almost self-evident. The importance that Von Ranke and those influenced by him placed upon the value of documentary sources necessitated extensive archival and bibliographical resources if historians were to perform their work successfully. If history was to emulate science the library and the archive must be its laboratory.

The period of intense nationalism that followed the French Revolution, and the awakened interest in history that developed from the Romantic movement promoted national responsibility for the archival preservation of historical records. In 1821 the École des Chartes for the training of historians in documentation was founded with a curriculum that emphasized history, languages, diplomatics, and paleography. By 1830 scholars began to join the archival staffs in numbers sufficient to raise the standards of archival work to a truly professional level. In 1838 the Public Records Office was established in England as the central archival agency of that country. In 1869 the British Historical Manuscripts Commission, proposed a decade earlier, was appointed, and began its effective work in the location, cataloging, and description of important manuscripts of public interest which were in the hands of private individuals.

The publication at this time of important documentary series has already been mentioned with reference to the German Monumenta, which were followed by other source collections such as Jaffe's Bibliotheca Rerum Germanicarum, Bohmer's Fontes Rerum Germanicarum, and other Fontes for Germany, Austria, Hungary, and elsewhere. In France, largely through the influence of the historian and statesman Guizot, committees for the publication of historical documents were organized and, with financial subvention from the government, published literally thousands of documents in hundreds of volumes, materials drawn from both Parisian and provincial archives. Again England lagged behind the Continent, but even there the publication of the Rolls Series was inaugurated in 1858, with the Chronicles, and five years later the Calendar of State Papers was begun. Calendaring is a descriptive techniques applicable to archival rather than to library practice. A calendar has been defined as "a chronologically arranged table of contents of all formal documents present in the original or in transcript in a collection or part of a collection."[9]

By the middle of the century the efforts of those who were urging the promotion of free, tax-supported public libraries both in England and the United States, were meeting with considerable success, and in this the popular enthusiasm for historical writing and the needs of professional historians for repositories of materials were conspicuous influences. Of these developments in America more will be said later, and for Great Britain it is sufficient here to point out that the Public Library Act was passed in 1850. The technical aspects of library economy, like archival practice under the influence of the École des Chartes, was making considerable headway. As early as 1839 the British Museum had adopted its so-called "ninety-one rules" for cataloging of its book collection and two years later they were published as the

British Museum. Dept. of Printed Books. Rules for Compiling the Catalogues of Printed Books, Maps and Music in the British Museum. Rev. ed. London: British Museum, printed by order of the Trustees, 1936. 67 pp.

From these rules were derived the Anglo-American cataloging practice of the present day, and even a century later our practice follows closely the basic principles set forth at that time. Such principles were devised to meet the needs of a large research collection in which many of the titles were unique and hence had to be identified exactly. Thus emerged a belief in the importance of minute bibliographic detail which in modern librarianship is useful only to a few research libraries, particularly the Library of Congress. But through the extensive use of L. C. cards these techniques have been absorbed into general li-

---

9
    S. Muller, J. A. Feith, and R. Fruin. Manual for the Arrangement and Description of Archives. (New York: H. W. Wilson Co., 1940), p. 165.

brary practice where they are not appropriate. The average library needs only enough description to enable it to identify a particular book within its own collection rather than in relation to the universe of books. Furthermore since 90 per cent of the holdings of most general libraries are composed of modern trade editions, such bibliographic detail is entirely irrelevant.

Contemporary Historiography: Toynbee, Spengler, Croce

The closing years of the nineteenth century and the early decades of the twentieth brought with them a reaction against Positivism, or more accurately, a revolt against the belief that science was the sum total of all knowledge. Negatively this implied a denial that history was a true science, which, as the movement attained maturity, became a positive affirmation that history was a true form of scholarship that differed from science but was nevertheless valid in its own right.

On the other hand, Toynbee, whose monumental Study of History is buttressed by an impressive display of erudition, restated the essential positivistic point of view. He divided history into unitary segments or "societies" of human activity -- Western Christendom, Hindu Society, Byzantine Christendom, Far Eastern Society, etc. The task of history, to him, involves the differentiation among these societies and the examination of the internal relationships within a given society itself. Certain societies are affiliated with other societies from which they are derived; others evince no such affiliation. Thus it becomes possible to arrange socieites according to this affiliation, classed in such ways as to exhibit the relationship of component characteristics. With such principles, derived obviously from the methodology of natural science, it becomes possible for Toynbee to undertake his real task, which is the comparative study of civilizations and the manner, methods, and reasons for their growth and decay.

In Germany, Spengler was even more positivistic than Toynbee. He too recognized in history a succession of self-contained "cultures" each with a character of its own but resembling the others in exhibiting an identical life cycle comparable to that of a living organism. Each culture begins in a state of barbarism, develops a political organization, artistic expression, and scientific achievements which flowers into a classical period, ultimately stagnates, decays, and sinks into a new stage of barbarism characterized by extreme commercialization. From this decadence nothing new emerges, the culture is dead and its creative power is exhausted. So precise is this cyclical movement that it becomes possible to foretell accurately the future of our own civilization by determining the point at which we stand on the curve. Such a morphological interpretation of history, based on external analysis, and claiming to foretell the future by the projection of scientific laws, was a complete denial of historical development as a mental process, an evolutionary movement in which the past is conserved in the present. Further Spengler did not hesitate to twist his data to support his interpretations, but The Decline of the West, for all its faults, and probably because of its prophetic nature seemingly supported by a vast accumulation of scholarship, was widely popular in both England and the United States.

In Italy Croce broke sharply with the positivist tradition by denying that history is a science at all. History, for Croce, is concerned with concrete individual facts, and the task of history is to narrate facts. An understanding of historical causation is the result of closer examination of the facts and comprehension of the relationships among them. Unlike his predecessors, who placed philosophy at the pinnacle of sciences, Croce subordinated philosophy to history in maintaining that philosophy was a constituent element within history (a universal element in a thought the concrete expression of which is individual). History is the knowledge of facts or events as they actually happened in their concrete individuality apprehended by the historian by "thinking himself into" the past until its life becomes his own. Science, on the other hand, is the external classification and analysis of facts.

Thus Croce asserted the autonomy of history by denying that it was subordinate to philosophy and affirming that it was secure against the encroachments of science. The philosophy of knowledge could not be imposed upon history because philosophical knowledge is a component part of all historical knowledge. Science is an objective and external rearrangement or reorientation of the facts of history, hence it cannot begin its analysis until history has supplied the materials essential to its operation. To Croce the scientific fact and the historic fact are synonymous, and until history has established facts, by its own independent investigation there can be no materials for the scientist to analyze and manipulate. It necessarily follows, then, that the subject matter of history is not the past as such, but that portion of the past for which historical evidence is obtainable. That which has perished cannot be relived or re-experienced in our own minds and hence does not exist as historic fact. That which is handed down to us by tradition becomes, for Croce, Chronicle, that which is believed upon testimony of others but is not known historically. History becomes chronicle when it is narrated by one who cannot relive the experiences he presents.

Bibliography

Greek Historiography

Herodotus. Herodotus, with an English translation by A. D. Godley. London: W. H. Heinemann; New York: G. D. Putnam's Sons, n. d. 4 v. (Half-title -- The Loeb Classical Library)

_____. The History of Herodotus. Translated by G. Rawlinson. London: J. M. Dent and Sons, 1933-37. (Half-title -- Everyman's Library)

Thucydides. The History of the Peloponnesian War. Translated by Rev. Henry Dale. London: G. Bell and Sons, 1896-1910. (Bohn's Classical Library)

_____. The Complete Writings of Thucydides. The Peloponnesian War. Translated by Crawley. New York: The Modern Library, 1934. (Half-title -- The Modern Library)

Roman Historiography

Polybius. The Histories, with an English translation by W. R. Paton. London: W. Heinemann; New York: Putnam's Sons, 1922-27. (Half-title -- The Loeb Classical Library)

Livius Titus. The History of Rome. London: J. M. Dent and Sons; New York: E. P. Dutton and Company, 1912-24. (Half-title -- Everyman's Library)

Tacitus Cornelius. The Complete Works of Tacitus. Translated by Alfred J. Church and William J. Bradribb, edited and with introduction by Moses Hadas. New York: The Modern Library, 1942. (Half-title -- The Modern Library)

Plutarchus. The Lives of the Noble Grecians and Romans. Translated by John Dryden and revised by Arthur H. Clough. New York: The Modern Library, 1932. (Half-title -- The Modern Library)

Medieval Historiography

Eusebius Pamphili, bp. of Caesarea. The Bodleian Manuscript of Jerome's Version of the Chronicle of Eusebius, reproduced in collotype. With an introduction by John Knight Fotheringham. Oxford: Clarendon Press, 1905.

Cassiodorus Senator, Flavius Magnus Aurelius. An Introduction to Divine and Human Readings, by Cassiodorus Senator; tr. with an introduction and notes by Leslie Webber Jones. New York: Columbia University Press, 1946. (Half-title -- Records of Civilization: Sources and Studies. A. P. Evans, editor. No. XL)

Beda Venerabilis. The Ecclesiastical History of the English Nation. With introduction by Vidor D. Scudder. London and Toronto: Dent; New York: Dutton, 1910. (Half-title -- Everyman's Library, ed. by Ernest Rhys. History)

Sullivan, Sir Edward. The Book of Kells... London and New York: "The Studio" ltd., 1920

Renaissance Historiography

Geoffrey of Monmouth. Histories of the Kings of Britain. Translated by Sebastian Evans ... London: J. M. Dent; New York: E. P. Dutton, 1911. (Half-title -- Everyman's Library. Ed. by Ernest Rhys. Romance. No. 5771)

Boccaccio, Giovanni. A Translation of Giovanni Boccaccio's Life of Dante; with an introduction and a note on the portraits of Dante by G. R. Carpenter. New York: Grolier Club, 1900.

Cavendish, George. The Life and Death of Thomas Wolsey. London: J. M. Dent and Sons, 1899. (Half-title -- The Temple Classics, ed. by Israel Gollancz)

Holinshed, Raphael. Holinshed Chronicle of England, Scotland, and Ireland ... London: J. Johnson, etc., 1807-08. 6 v.

> NOTE: A modern work on the history of librarianship, which is annalistic in character, is worth noting here. It demonstrates well that no type of history is limited to a single period, but that when the histories of particular fields or places first become of interest the development of historical writing is quite likely to follow the same pattern as that of general history. Annals marshall facts in the simplest order, that of chronology, as a prerequisite to more interpretative treatments. This book is also useful in following the development of libraries through the succeeding periods of history:

Thornton, John Leonard. The Chronology of Librarianship; an introduction to the history of libraries and book-collecting. London: Grafton, 1941.

Descartes and the Age of Reason

Descartes, René. A Discourse on Method. London and Toronto: J. M. Dent; New York: Dutton, 1912. (Half-title -- Everyman's Library, ed. by Ernest Rhys. Philosophy and Theology)

Montesquieu, Charles Louis de Secondat, baron de la Brede et de The Spirit of Laws. With d'Alembert's analysis of the work. Tr. from the French, by Thomas Nugent ... New ed., rev. with additional notes, and a new memoir from the latest French editions, by J. V. Prichard ... London: G. Bell, 1914. 2 v. (Half-title -- Bohn's Standard Library)

Gibbon, Edward. The History of the Decline and Fall of the Roman Empire. Ed. in seven volumes with introduction, notes, appendices, and index by J. B. Bury ... London: Methuen and Company, 1900-1902; New York: The Modern Library, n. d. (Modern Library Giant, 2 v.)

Anti-Cartesianism

Vico, Giovanni Battista. The New Science of Giambattista Vico. Tr. from the 3rd ed. 1744, by Thomas Goddard Bergin and Max Harold Fisch. Ithaca, New York: Cornell University Press, 1948.

Naudé, Gabriel. News from France; or a description of the library of Cardinal Mazarin, preceded by "The Surrender of the Library" (now newly translated), two tracts written by G. Naudé. Chicago: A. C. McClurg and Company, 1907. (Added t. p. Literature of libraries in the seventeenth and eighteenth centuries. Ed. by J. C. Dana and H. W. Kent)

The Beginnings of Scientific History

Percy, Thomas. Reliques of Ancient English Poetry ... London: Dent; New York: Dutton, 1910. (Half-title -- Everyman's Library, ed. by Ernest Rhys)

Rousseau, Jean Jacques. A Discourse Upon the Origin and Foundation of the Inequality Among Mankind. London: Dodsley, 1761.

Herder, Johann Gottfried von. Outlines of a Philosophy of the History of Man. Translated from the German of John Godfrey Herder, by T. Churchill ... London: Printed for J. Johnson. by K. Hansard, 1803.

Grimm, Jakob Ludwig Karl. Folk-lore and Fable; Aesop, Grimm, Andersen, with introductions, notes and illustrations. New York: P. F. Collier and Son, c. 1909.

The New History: Niebuhr and Ranke

Niebuhr, Barthold Georg. The History of Rome. Translated by Julius Charles Hare and Connap Thirlwall ... London: Wallon and Maberly, 1855-60.

Ranke, Leopold von. History of the Popes, Their Church and State ... tr. by E. Fowler, with a special introduction by William Clark. Rev. ed. New York: P. F. Collier, c. 1901. (Half-title -- The World's Greatest Literature)

_____. A History of England Principally in the Seventeenth Century. Oxford: Clarendon Press, 1875.

Macaulay, Thomas Babington Macaulay. History of England. London: Dent; New York: Dutton, n. d. 3 v. (Everyman's Library)

Carlyle, Thomas. The French Revolution; a History. London: Dent; New York: Dutton, 1914, 1913. (Half-title -- Everyman's Library, ed. by Ernest Rhys. History)

_____. Oliver Cromwell, with a selection from his letters and speeches abridged and newly edited. London: Hutchinson, 1905. (Half-title -- The Library of Standard Biography)

Froude, James Anthony. Thomas Carlyle; a History of His Life in London, 1834-1881. New York: Scribner, 1884.

The Influence of Nineteenth Century Science

Buckle, Henry Thomas. History of Civilization in England ... From the 2d London ed., to which is added an alphabetical index. New York: Appleton-Century Company, 1934.

Taine, Hippolyte Adolphe. History of English Literature. Tr. from the French by Henry Van Laun, with a special introduction by J. Scott Clark. Rev. ed. New York: The Colonial Press, c. 1900.

Institutional, Social, and Economic History

Guizot, Francois Pierre Guillaume. General History of Civilization in Europe. Ed. with critical and supplementary notes, by George Wells Knight. New York: Appleton, 1907.

Fustel de Coulanges, Numa Denis. The Ancient City; A Study on the Religion, Laws, and Institutions of Greece and Rome ... tr. by Willard Small. 12th ed. Boston: Lathrop, Lee and Shepard Co., (1920)

Hallam, Henry. Constitutional History of England, Henry VII to George II. London: Dent; New York: Dutton, 1912. (Half-title -- Everyman's Library, ed. by Ernest Rhys. History, No. 621-623)

Kemble, John Mitchell. The Saxons in England. A History of the English Commonwealth till the Period of the Norman Conquest ... A new ed. by Walter De Gray Birch. London: B. Quaritch, 1876.

Vinagradoff, Paul. Roman Law in Medieval Europe. London and New York: Harper, 1909. (Half-title -- Harper's Library of Living Thought)

Maitland, Frederick William. The Constitutional History of England, a course of lectures delivered by F. W. Maitland ... Cambridge: The University Press, 1931.

Bodin, Jean. Method for the Easy Comprehension of History. Tr. by Beatrice Reynolds. New York: Columbia University Press, 1945.

Schmoller, Gustav. The Mercantile System and Its Historical Significance Illustrated Chiefly from Prussian History ... New York: P. Smith, 1931.

Cunningham, William. The Growth of English Industry and Commerce. Cambridge: The University Press, 1922-29.

Scott, William Robert. The Constitution and Finance of English,
   Scottish and Irish Joint-Stock Companies to 1720. Cambridge:
   The University Press, 1910-12.

Unwin, George. Industrial Organization in the Sixteenth and Seventeenth
   Centuries. Oxford: Clarendon Press, 1904.

_____. The Gilds and Companies of London. London: Methuen, (1908)

Contemporary Historiography

Toynbee, Arnold Joseph. A Study of History ... Abridgment of vol.
   1-5 by D. C. Somervell ... New York and London: Oxford University
   Press, 1947.

Spengler, Oswald. The Decline of the West ... New York: A. A. Knopf,
   1939. 2 v. in 1. "Authorized translation with notes by Charles
   Francis Atkinson."

Croce, Benedetto. History as the Story of Liberty. Translated from the
   Italian by Sylvia Sprigge. New York: W. W. Norton, (1941)

CHAPTER IV

AMERICAN HISTORIOGRAPHY

The Colonial Period

The writing of history in America is here treated separately,
not because it was isolated from the main stream of historical
writing in England and on the Continent, but because it represents
a natural and homogeneous unit in which European tendencies and
influences were shaped and molded by conditions in the New World.
In the second place, the American librarian will naturally be concerned primarily with American history and should be more familiar with American writers and titles than with those of other countries.

American historical writing during the Colonial period was
deeply rooted in the Renaissance and the Reformation. From the
Middle Ages it derived a theological orientation and the zeal to direct history or chronicle to a didactic end. But over all lay the
influence of the Colonial environment, giving to it a new and different meaning, a raison d'être, that set it apart from similar endeav-
ors in the rest of the Western hemisphere. Much of the writing during these early decades was not consciously history, but rather
record -- valuable record -- which through the passing of time has
acquired great historical meaning and significance.

During the seventeenth century the writers of history were, in
every instance, transplanted Englishmen who had retained their admiration and affection for their mother country and were relatively
untouched by the conditions of life in the New World. They wrote
with a practical purpose; to tell the folks back home about the new
continent, either in formal reports to colonial management groups
or in tracts to promote migration across the Atlantic; to defend or
attack the course of events in the British Colonies; or to strengthen
the courage of the settlers themselves, who were finding that the
perils of the wilderness were almost too great for human fortitude.
The writings of these men, who were always either clergymen or
men of action, were limited in scope to the geographic area with
which they were immediately familiar, and restricted to contemporary events with which they had direct personal contact. Often
they were autobiographical, based largely upon personal experi-

ence and conversations with contemporaries. In form they tended
to be annalistic, and much of the writing was set down without
thought of publication.

The first person in America to write a book was that bragging,
swaggering man of action, Captain John Smith, who is popularly best
remembered because he linked his name with that of Pocahontas,
after she was safely dead, and thus gave to this country its first
folk tale. Ridiculed by Justin Winsor and Henry Adams and praised
by Samuel Elliott Morison, John Smith as a historian has always
been a controversial figure. Though his reputation has improved
with the passing of time, posterity will certainly never regard him
as highly as he esteemed himself. Often he is as much interested
in the geographical terrain, the flora and the fauna of Virginia, as
in the events that took place there. Though his writings are a sorry
mixture of fact and fancy, he still remains one of the best sources
of information concerning the first years of British colonization
along the Atlantic coast.

During this same century New England gave to American historical writing two documents of outstanding importance -- William
Bradford's History of Plymouth Plantation and the Journal of John
Winthrop. Both were prominent figures in the public life of the
Bay area, and both were concerned with essentially the same period
of our colonial development. Bradford, who might rightly be regarded as the true father of American historiography, represents
more nearly the point of view of the "common man," the typical
Pilgrim who knew all too well the hardships of the early years of
the Plymouth settlement. He had no definite theories of liberty,
government, or the church, no axe to grind, no special defense of
the Pilgrims. But he was a profoundly religious man, a cloth-
maker descended from the English yeomanry, with a real gift for
simple and vivid prose that recreates, even after the passage of
three centuries, a lasting picture of Colonial New England. Though
the manuscript was not written for publication and much of it was
set down long after the events narrated had passed, it is a deeply
moving and beautiful account that, more than any other work, has
given to the Pilgrims and their colony the distinctive place which
they hold in American history and folklore.

By contrast, John Winthrop was university-trained and a member
of the Inner Temple, a leader and ruler of men to whom others naturally turned for direction. Convinced of the rightness of his position
and the divine mission of the Puritan experiment, he has set down in
his Journal the day-to-day account of the struggles and problems of
establishing a new commonwealth in a not too hospitable wilderness.
Winthrop's accounts are less readable than Bradford's, but probably
more valuable to later historians because of their nearness to the
events they narrate. In common with most journals of men in public
life they are, of necessity, less full during those periods when their
author was most active.

The third quarter of the seventeenth century was a relatively

sterile period in American historical writing. The first generation
of writers, mainly college men trained in England, were being replaced by younger men, trained at Harvard, or without formal
college instruction, who lacked the ability and religious zeal of their
predecessors and contributed little to the writing of history. Further,
it was a period of strife with the ever-present Indian, King Philip's
War, that left little opportunity for contemplative activity. With the
close of the century, however, came the Mather dynasty and a new
era in American historiography.

In 1676, Increase Mather wrote his Brief History of the War
with the Indians, a chronicle of King Philip's War that emphasized
the picturesque and the sensational, wherein he expressed the need
for a true "History of New England," a task which he left to his son.
His Remarkable Providences was compiled from the replies to an
inquiry made of all ministers of the region requesting examples,
drawn from personal experience, illustrating the power of God's favor.
Thus he anticipated the questionnaire method of modern social science, but his selections were often more sensational than historically accurate. Probably his greatest contribution to historical
writing was the interest he inspired in his son, Cotton, for historical investigation.

The Mathers were truly a remarkable family, and though the
dynasty reached the height of its power in Cotton, four generations
passed before it went completely to seed. Of all the figures in
American history probably Cotton is the most difficult to appraise
without bias. Certainly he was a sensationalist and an arch-pedant,
yet his widespread reputation as a remarkable scholar and a great
man of God was not unfounded, even though such worship made of
him an insufferable prig. A child without a childhood, he entered
Harvard at the age of eleven, a "literary behemoth," the bibliography
of whose writings runs to more than four hundred titles, a man with
a prodigious memory, a vast store-house of academic learning.
Probably only Jonathan Edwards and Benjamin Franklin can compare with him in breadth of knowledge. In 1693 he set about the
writing of a general church history of New England, the Magnalia
Christi Americana, which was completed four years later. This
monumental work, which is one of the most influential books in
American historiography, encompasses an account of the planting
of the New England colonies, the biographies of governors, mag-
istrates, and the most famous divines, a history of Harvard College
and an account of some of its graduates, a general ecclesiastical
history, "remarkable providences," and a final section on "the Wars
of the Lord " Repetitious, filled with homilies on proper conduct and
accounts of strange revelations, buttressed by both documents and old
wives' tales, often unreliable and impregnated with prejudice, one can
say of it as has been said of his Diary, that it is a combination of the
Apocalypse, Pilgrim's Progress, and Alice in Wonderland. He
bitterly attacked the Quakers, and had only contempt and hatred for
the "heathen Indians," who seemed to resent God's plan to establish

60

His kingdom in the wilderness. Yet he had access to many important documents and sources of historical information that have long since been lost, and his curious compilation remains an important source for Colonial history.

Many of the characteristics of historical writing during the seventeenth century continued through the eighteenth to the eve of the American Revolution, though with the passing of the Mather influence the writing became less dominantly theological. The influence of the Indian remained a prominent factor and the work begun by Mary Rowlandson, Daniel Gookin, Captain John Mason, and Colonel Benjamin Church, was continued in the writings of Samuel Penhallow and Cadwallader Colden. The most prominent diarist was Samuel Sewall. Formal biographies also began to appear; Samuel Mather wrote of his distinguished father, John Norton wrote of John Cotton, and Benjamin Franklin began the preparation of his Autobiography. Travel accounts and descriptions of the country also began to appear, Crevecoeur's Letters from an American Farmer, William Byrd's History of the Dividing Line Between Virginia and North Carolina, and John Lawson, Surveyor General of North Carolina, published an ... Exact Description and Natural History of that Country.

In short, one might summarize this new temper in American historiography by saying that it was far more mundane in subject matter and that the secular influence was steadily increasing, but that historical writing was still largely local in scope and in point of view. American historical writing evinced no such philosophical and comprehensive approach as was characteristic of contemporaneous work across the Atlantic, nor did the meager library resources of the Colonies permit extensive use of documentation. Historical writing along the eastern coast was still largely personal because there were no great collections of material to support the work of a Gibbon, a Hume, or a Robertson. But it was beginning to achieve some measure of objectivity. The earlier fear of the Indian was slowly passing, and at times he even began to assume the position of the "noble savage." Colden showed a real sympathy for the Five Nations, and Lawson, who ironically was tortured and killed by the red men, showed a real understanding of their unpleasant situation.

Samuel Sewall, whose diary covers the years from 1675 to 1729, stands at a transition point between the earlier colonial historiography and the later. Torn between the old Puritanism and the new age, and greatly troubled by the conflict, Sewall, who was a lover of fine foods and good living, illustrates the coming of the middle-class mind and the rise of commercialization. With a Pepysian genius for self-revelation he records even the smallest details of his life.

Of those who wrote formal history during this period the names of William Stith, Thomas Prince, and Thomas Hutchinson are preeminent. William Stith, member of the Randolph family, Oxford graduate and a governor of William and Mary College, wrote history that, for its scholarship and accuracy, ranks with the best produced

61

during the Colonial period. Convinced that it was the responsibility of contemporary historians to make full use of the historical materials before they were lost to future generations, he had, because of his position in public life, access to many important papers and he made extensive use of such materials, especially the records of the London Company. Though he achieved an astonishing degree of factual accuracy, his great fault lay in an almost complete absence of a sense of proportion, with the result that his writings become a mass of detail. His projected monumental history of Virginia was completed only through the first quarter of the seventeenth century, largely because the Virginia reading public was not equal to the support of so ambitious an undertaking.

The name of Thomas Prince is still one to inspire respect and admiration. He possessed the true historian's mind, a high standard of scholarship, a healthy skepticism toward the authenticity of his sources, a point of view as scientific as that of any modern investigator. "I cite my vouchers to every passage; and I have done my utmost, first to find out the truth, and then to relate it in the clearest order. I have labored after accuracy ... " Like Stith he was convinced that the historian should feel responsible for the preservation of materials that might later be lost, and though he, too, incorporated much detail in his Chronological History of New England, unlike the historian of Virginia, he wrote with sprightliness and vigor. A pastor of the South Church in Boston, he is reminiscent of the medieval historians in beginning his Chronology with the creation of Adam, "year one, first month, sixth day," and continues his chronology through the birth of Christ, and Columbus' arrival to the New World to the "discovery of New England by Captain Gosnold." His devotion to the unadorned fact, and his use of materials later lost (the manuscript of Bradford's history of Plymouth was in his private library until the Revolutionary War) made his work an important source for later historians even though it was never carried beyond the year 1633. A half-century later John Pintard wrote to Jeremy Belknap, "I shall do pretty well as long as Prince holds out, but shall be at a loss after I part with him."

The writing of history was, for Thomas Hutchinson, but one activity in a life dedicated to public service, and his three volume History of the Colony of Massachusetts Bay, from 1628 to 1774, exhibits both the strength and the weakness that derive from an active political life. As lieutenant governor, governor, and chief justice, he was an active participant in much of the history about which he wrote, and his official position gave him ready access to documentary materials. But his writing and research suffered from constant interruption, history was often but a peripheral activity, even to the point at which it was impossible "to write two sheets at a sitting." Despite a strong tendency toward conservatism the first two volumes of his work, 1628 to 1750, are remarkably dispassionate and judicial in their interpretation, even to the treatment

of his great-grandmother, Anne Hutchinson. But the concluding
volume, which covers the years of his own active participation in
public affairs, is much more biased, and also much more interesting. Further, the demands of an active life often left him insuf-
ficient time to examine and evaluate sources that might have corrected
some of his errors in judgment, and frequently important new discoveries of material were crowded into foot-notes because there was in-
sufficient time to incorporate them in the previously written text.
But for all his shortcomings and personal predispositions, his organization of materials and soundness of judgment are far superior
to those of most of his contemporaries. His analysis of the origins
of the Revolution evinced greater objectivity than was displayed by
any succeeding historian for almost a century.

Such, in broadest outline, was the course of American historical
writing during the Colonial years. J. Franklin Jameson called it
"the heroic age;" to Allan Nevins, it was "the period of the primitive."
There is truth in both points of view. Certainly it was not great historical writing in the sense that European historiography was great,
nor was it widely influential as was such writing in Germany and
France. Much of it was pretentious, bombastic, and didactic.
Written to support a thesis, to prove a position, to justify a way of
life, it was of the same tough fibre as the colonial mind itself. At
once both primitive and heroic, its polemics of theological and
political controversy were the very foundations of our American
culture.

The extremely meager Colonial library resources of the seventeenth century were substantially augmented in the eighteenth century. The book collections of Harvard College were still the most
important, but the establishment of printing presses along the eastern seaboard and increasing importations of books from across the
Atlantic facilitated the beginnings of a real library development. The
founding of other colonial colleges, William and Mary, Yale, Princeton, Columbia, Pennsylvania, Brown, Rutgers, and Dartmouth, improved academic library resources. [1] At the turn of the century
modest "town" book collections were set up in scattered communities
and from England the Reverend Thomas Bray was active in sending
books to the Anglican parishes of colonial America. In Philadelphia,
during the fourth decade of the eighteenth century, Benjamin Franklin
inaugurated the Philadelphia Library Company, a voluntary association of individuals who pooled their modest financial resources to
purchase books for the use of the group. This type of "public" library spread rapidly in metropolitan centers along the Atlantic coast,
especially in the New England states. [2] Not many years thereafter

---

[1]

Louis Shores. Origins of the American College Library. (N. Y.:
Barnes and Noble, 1935). 290 pp.

[2]

J. H. Shera. Foundations of the Public Library. (Chicago:
Univ. of Chicago Press, 1949) Chaps. III and IV.

early "circulating," i. e., rental libraries, were established by en-
terprising merchants who sought profit from exploiting popular reading
tastes. [3] Also, important private libraries were formed. [4] The private
library of Thomas Prince, now in the Boston Public Library, is still
a significant collection of early Americana. In the South the private
book collections of wealthy landowners were particularly noteworthy,
one of the most important being that of William Byrd II, of Westover,
Virginia. At this same period James Logan of Philadelphia began the
accumulation of his library, which was later consolidated with that
of the Philadelphia Library Company. [5] Thomas Jefferson was busily
purchasing books which, after the War of 1812, were purchased by
the United States for the Library of Congress. [6] Importation still
remained the great source of book supply, but printing and publishing
in America were definitely on the increase. The important fact is
that, as the edge of the wilderness receded westward and as more
stable economic and social conditions were established, American
culture became more and more bookish. [7]

The Period of the Republic, 1776-1820

The advent of the Revolutionary War marks a definite change in
American historical writing. From the British historical writers
were derived certain tendencies that colored American historiography.
Primarily there was a shift from Tory to Whig emphasis, and the
point of view was more urban, industrial, and mercantile, but it
was not fundamentally democratic in spirit. As in the writings of
Burke and Hallam there was pride in a slow but orderly process of
change, though there was an almost panicky fear of the radicalism of
Thomas Paine. Certainly it was ultra-nationalistic, prompted primarily by the impact of war. From the romantic movement was derived an emphasis on the Gothic, a recognition of the worth of the
primitive, and a return to the admiration of the past. An implicit

---

[3]
Shera. Op. Cit. Chap. V.

[4]
Carl L. Cannon. American Book Collectors and Collecting from
Colonial Times to the Present. (N. Y.: H. W. Wilson, 1941). 391 pp.

[5]
Austin K. Gray. Benjamin Franklin's Library. (N. Y.: Macmillan,
1937). 80 pp.

[6]
David C. Mearns. The Story up to Now, The Library of Congress,
1800-1946. (Washington, D. C.: Library of Congress, 1947). 226 pp.

[7]
Hellmut Lehmann-Haupt, and others. The Book in America.
(N. Y.: R. R. Bowker, 1951). 493 pp.
Lawrence C. Wroth. The Colonial Printer. (Portland, Me.:
Southworth-Anthoensen Press, 1938). 368 pp.

rebellion against excessive emphasis on style was accompanied by
an increased skepticism of sources, and finally there was, throughout,
the basic influence of the evangelical revival in the Church.

American historical writings during this period fall into four
major groups: (a) histories of the Revolution; (b) biographies (especially of the Revolutionary worthies); (c) state histories; and (d)
collections of historical source materials.

(a) The first group are practically worthless today except as they
reveal the temper of the historical mind of the time. Plagiarism was
rife, especially from the British Annual Register, even when the
authors happened to be eye-witnesses of events which they were nar-
rating.

(b) In biography the outstanding work is John Marshall's Life of
George Washington, in which the author tried to do for his subject
what Beveridge later did for Marshall himself. The work received
universal praise but, though Marshall knew Washington intimately,
much of his book was taken from British sources, especially from
the Annual Register, and Marshall's claim to have cited all his
sources is plain deceit. As a result his work is in effect a British
history of the Washington era, though its author could profitably have
drawn heavily from his own experience. Far more popular in its appeal was Parson Weems' Life of Washington, which was sold throughout the length and breadth of the land by itinerant book peddlers, including Weems himself, and is supposed to have been published in
as many as seventy editions. Weems was a careless biographer and
a thoroughly inaccurate historian, but he had an eye for the colorful,
and his enthusiasm for the virtues of industry, temperance, and
frugality increased the popularity of his work. It was he who gave
us the cherry tree invention --

"George,"said his father, "do you know who killed that beautiful little cherry tree yonder in the garden?" This was a tough
question; and George staggered under it for a moment ... "I
can't tell a lie, Pa, you know I can't tell a lie. I did cut it with
my hatchet." "Run to my arms, you dearest boy," cried his
father in transports ... "glad am I, George, that you killed my
tree; for you have paid for it a thousand fold. Such an act of
heroism in my son is more worth than a thousand trees, though
blossomed with silver, and their fruits of purest gold."

This bit of fiction is equalled only by the story of John Smith and
Pocahontas, and is probably known to more people than the
Declaration of Independence, the Constitution, or the Gettysburg
address. The popularity of Weems' blending of biography, morality,
and oratory tells one more about the spirit of the new nation than
volumes of historical exposition.

(c) State histories represent an American phase of the emphasis
on nationalism in England, and we can perceive in them the beginnings

of the comprehensive historical writing that flourished in the 1830's.
In the early years of the nineteenth century the states attained the
end of a natural period in their history, and the time was right for
a retrospective appraisal of their progress. Hewatt's history of
South Carolina and Georgia, Proud's History of Pennsylvania,
Benjamin Trumbull's history of Connecticut, and John Daly Burk's
History of Virginia, are typical. But by far the most significant
figure in the field of early history was Jeremy Belknap. This historian of New Hampshire, who was an impecunious preacher at
Dover, bought at a great personal sacrifice long files of newspapers,
made the fullest use of every possible contact to gain access to official papers, and enlisted the invaluable assistance of his intimate
friend Ebenezer Hazard, then Postmaster General, in the assembly
of materials. His History of New Hampshire remains the definitive
treatment of New Hampshire history, so closely does it approximate
the standards of modern historical scholarship. His biographical
dictionary, American Biography, the materials for which had begun
to accumulate during his work on the New Hampshire volumes, was
the forerunner of a long line of such compilations culminating in the
Dictionary of American Biography. The correspondence with Hazard
is not only delightful reading, but is filled with much important social
history and an admirable presentation of the troubles that beset a
writer of history in the late eighteenth century. No less important
than his own historical investigations was the enthusiasm for history
that he inspired in others. Not only did he successfully enlist the
aid of many in the collection and preservation of important materials,
but he was largely responsible for the formation of the Massachusetts
Historical Society, the first of its kind in this country.

    (d) Among those individuals who were amassing documents for the
use of later historians Ebenezer Hazard has already been mentioned.
His contract with Congress for the collection of archival materials
was never fulfilled, but he did publish a two-volume collection of
Colonial documents, and his son Samuel carried out the traditions of
the father by collecting Pennsylvania archival materials. [8] Hezekiah
Niles, best known for his association with Niles' Register (a good example of an early weekly journal, still much used in research), began
work on his Principles and Acts of the Revolution, and Jonathan
Elliot was engaged in assembling debates in the state constitutional
conventions. Peter Force, who regarded the collection of documents
as a source of income rather than as a scholarly activity (but who also drove his wife nearly to distraction with the masses of materials
he accumulated) assembled, with the aid of a grant from Congress,
materials for the publication of a national archive series to be modeled
after similar publications in France and England. At about this same
time Gales and Seaton were also engaged by Congress to publish the
American State Papers. Jared Sparks, one-time owner and editor of

---

8
    See Reading (by Carter).

the North American Review, became interested in collecting the
papers of Washington and Franklin, and thus is to be remembered
as more a collector and editor of documents than as a formal
historian. In this growing popular interest in history, and the increasing enthusiasm for the preservation of historical records,
the foundation was being laid for the distinguished work of the
"middle group" of American Historians.

Mid-Nineteenth Century American Historiography

The intensification of the spirit of American nationalism, resulting from two military victories over the mother country; a
concurrent urge to tell the world about the achievements of the new
Republic; the achievement of historical perspective on the events
surrounding the Revolution; the growth of a wealthy patronage that
could support historical investigation; the slow but steady accumulation of library resources, both private and institutional, and the
accumulation of archival materials essential to competent historical work; the voluntary association of schools for cooperative attack upon historical problems; the appearance of periodical publication that gave to the historian a medium for the dissemination of
the results of his inquiries; and the rapid expansion of a reading
public that was interested in historical writing, all contributed to
the flowering of historical scholarship that characterized the middle decades of the nineteenth century.
  With the work of Prescott, Parkman, Bancroft, and Hildreth
historical writing in America became popular to an unprecedented
degree. It was a broad, exploring type of history, often characterized by intensity of feeling, both religious and political. Politics
was rapidly becoming a national pastime as well as a profession
and party lines were sharply drawn. It was both democratic and
Democratic; it "voted for Jackson on every page." Over all lay
the prevailing faith in progress, a conviction that the new
Republic possessed unlimited resources for growth and improvement. History became philosophic and idealistic; historians concerned themselves with the eternal verities of right and wrong,
and hence could pronounce unqualified judgments concerning religion, politics, and social problems. Such a point of view did not
create balanced historical interpretation, but it certainly made for
popularity.
  To Bancroft American history was a heroic epic, an exultation
over American achievement, a credo of faith in eternal national
progress. The great exemplar of "drum and trumpet" history, his
monumental History of the United States, reads like a Fourth of
July oration, but the public loved it and he became America's historian as ·Longfellow had become her poet. Though he made ex-

tensive use of manuscript materials, gave citations, and was accurate in his statement of facts, he did not hesitate to suppress materials that failed to contribute to his didactic purpose, and his interpretation is today completely discredited. Though he could "sell" history to the populace, he lacked historical insight into the development of our national psychology, and did not perceive the complexities of our national growth. Economic and social history were almost completely excluded from his work. To him the Revolution was the spontaneous uprising of thirteen united colonies. This very heroic interpretation gave to his work its tremendous influence. At that time his was incomparably the best of the few general American histories, and as a synthesis it represented the accumulation of hundreds of individual works. Not only did his volumes find their way into "one-third of the homes of the Nation," they profoundly influenced the text-book presentation of American history for generations to come.

In contrast, Richard Hildreth stands out in opposition to Bancroft's rabid democracy. He was the "Federalist facing Democrat, fact against rhapsody, dull precise prose against turbulent windy rhetoric." His writing is probably biased for the cause of Federalism as Bancroft's was for Jacksonian Democracy, but it was written with competent, matter-of-fact hardheadedness, and therefrom stems its value. He strove to present the founders of the American nation, "unbedaubed with patriotic rouge, wrapped up in no fine-spun cloaks of excuses and apology, without stilts, buskins, tinsel, or bedizement, in their own proper persons, often rude, hard, narrow, superstitious, and mistaken, but always earnest, downright, manly, and sincere." An anti-romantic in an age of romanticism, Hildreth exhibited many of the characteristics that became part of the creed of twentieth century American historians.

John G. Palfrey, in the tradition of Sparks and Bancroft, wrote history to glorify the Fathers of the Republic, to record the conquest of a vast continent, to praise the achievement of religious and political freedom, and to present the Revolution as a conflict between "patriots" and "tyrants". His five-volume history of New England is a glorification of the "worthies" who guided the destinies of that region, who could do no wrong, and who left as their most precious heritage the memory of "their wise and steady virtue."

Three historians of this period, Prescott, Parkman, and Motley, emphasized the dramatic element in history. The outstanding characteristic of Prescott's work is its author's ability to give color and descriptive brilliance to historical narration. Strongly influenced by the work of Washington Irving, Prescott's histories of Mexico and Peru are the work of a gregarious spirit who loved danger and excitement, but who because of a physical handicap (he was almost blind) was compelled to seek adventure vicariously in the records of history. Greatly aided by Edward Everett in the collection of Spanish documents, he laboriously made use of such sources, but today his work survives largely because of the vividness of its presentation.

In contrast to Prescott, John L. Motley was a man of radiant health and abundant energy. Motley, the least able of the three, was a member of the merchant class, an aristocrat who saw in the Dutch burger a reflection of the Boston merchant. He chose to write history of the Netherlands, not only because it exemplified the triumph of Protestantism over Catholicism, but because in the rise of the Dutch Republic he saw a parallel with the rise of the republic of the United States. Though he lacked the style and color of Prescott and Parkman, he took more liberties than they with factual presentation. William the Silent was always right, the Duke of Alva always wrong.

Not only was Francis Parkman the most able of these three men, but to many he still stands as the best historian this country has ever produced. He was a rare combination of true historical scholarship and a fine literary style. He chose to do for Canadian history what Prescott had tried to do for the countries to the south. Though a New Englander he was completely untouched by the provincialism of that region. His treatment of the Anglo-French conflict for the control of North America is rooted in the romantic school of historical writing, but his indefatigable use of documentary sources and his sound scholarship have given his work lasting value. From The Oregon Trail to Montcalm and Wolfe, his finest work, stretch almost forty years of industrious historical scholarship against a constant battle with poor eyesight and ill health. To say that his history neglected the social and economic forces is to condemn him for failure to use materials that were not available. To be sure, his point of view was sympathetic to the British, but he was not anti-Catholic nor was he an incurable romantic. Only in minor detail has modern scholarship improved upon his work. He was the first to recognize seriously the importance of geography to history, and the effect of the West upon our historical development. His works strongly influenced the writing of Theodore Roosevelt, and, though he had little importance in Turner's philosophy, both are a part of the same developmental sequence. Though rooted in the romantic tradition, he could rise above it to construct an historical panorama of permanent value. He is as John Fiske said, "Of all American historians ... the most deeply and peculiarly American, yet, ... at the same time the broadest and most cosmopolitan."

The period from 1790 to the eve of the Civil War was one of unprecedented library and archival development in the United States. Only this development made available the non-American materials which such writers as Prescott and Motley needed in their break with the earlier parochialism of American history. The founding of the Massachusetts Historical Society in 1791, and of the American Antiquarian Society in 1812, were both symptomatic of the spirit of the period and an encouragement to similar undertakings in other

states. The Library of Congress was established in 1800, though
several decades elapsed before it became of great importance as a
national library. Other states followed the leadership of Massachusetts in creating state libraries. The Boston Athenaeum, which
emerged from a publishing venture during the first decade of the
nineteenth century, soon grew, under the leadership of William
Smith Shaw, to be one of the most important collections of its time.
American scholars travelled extensively in Europe and brought back
an intense enthusiasm for European library resources, and an eagerness to see similar developments on this side of the Atlantic. Fisher
Ames' lament that there were not enough books in the whole of the
United States to supply the materials for such a work as Gibbon's
was taken up as a battle cry by those who were pushing for improved
library resources, and John Quincy Adams began to collect, at his
own expense, the titles necessary for the verification of Gibbon's
citations. George Ticknor assembled, at his great house in Boston,
one of the finest private libraries of that period, a library which
grew out of his Wanderjahre in Europe. [9] The interest in the preservation of archival materials has already been mentioned, and
some work was begun in the publication of American historical documents.

Almost from the beginning the public library was regarded by
its promoters as the fountain-head of the historical source materials of scholarship. Edward Everett saw this as the main purpose
of the newly-established Boston Public Library, and even George
Ticknor who, more than his contemporaries, emphasized the importance of libraries in the improvement of popular culture, acknowledged that a substantial portion of the library collections should
be composed of materials of value to present and future historians.
Enthusiasm for popular libraries supported by public funds, was
encouraged by many groups in the community: laborers, merchants,
mechanics, as well as the professional classes. In 1833 Peterborough,
New Hampshire, became the first municipality to vote public funds
for the creation of a public library, and in 1849 New Hampshire became the first state to authorize municipalities to use public funds
for the founding of town book collections. Such were the modest
beginnings of an American public library movement which was to
make its first major advance with the birth of the Boston Public
Library in the sixth decade of the century. Librarians were becoming professionally conscious, and in 1853 an abortive attempt
was made to form a professional library association, an effort which
did not meet with permanent success until twenty-five years later.

At long last there seemed some hope for the realization of
Ticknor''s dream of American pre-eminence in librarianship. By
1876 libraries had become so numerous that it was possible to es-

---

9
Described in Chapter IV of Van Wyck Brooks' Flowering of
New England (New York: Dutton, 1937). 550 pp.

tablish a permanent professional organization on a solid foundation, and to begin the publication of the Library Journal, the first American journal devoted exclusively to library interests. Practices within libraries had become sufficiently complex as to require some kind of standardization. As we have seen, there had already been attempts to codify cataloging practice, and in 1876 Cutter published his Rules for a Printed Dictionary Catalogue,[10] the first American formulation to win general acceptance, and still the foundation of contemporary cataloging practice. Also in this same year appeared the first edition of Melvil Dewey's Decimal Classification. The treatment of history obviously reflects the academic view of history prevalent at that period. Thus the 900's include "Geography and travel" and "Biography" as well as formal history, whereas the history of a particular subject is classified with the subject to which it relates. The 900's, as originally conceived, were restricted largely to political history, but today they have tended to become a residual class for the incorporation of materials which do not fit under more specific headings. For instance, the history of religious sects is classified in the 200's; histories of commerce, of transportation, or of political parties would fall in the 300's; histories of languages in the 400's; histories of medicine, of agriculture, or of manufacturing in the 600's; histories of architecture, town planning or photography in the 700's; and histories of literature in the 800's.

Two principles of classification are operative in the history class, place and time. Basically history is divided into the dichotomy of ancient and modern, with appropriate geographic subdivisions under each. Modern history, for example, is subdivided first by continent and later by country, with temporal subdivisions where necessary. In certain places, notably the United States, such subdivision is carried to specific localities, e. g., Chicago, 977.11. Subsequent alteration of political boundaries, the rise to political importance of powers which in 1876 played a relatively unimportant part in world history, e. g., Russia, and the tendency to view history from a regional rather than a strictly political viewpoint have all contributed to the obsolescence of the Dewey tables and multiplied the problems of classification in this area.

The dominance of the political view of history in the 900's also accounts for the inclusion of the biographies of royal personages

---

10
Charles A. Cutter. Rules for a Printed Dictionary Catalogue. (Washington: Government Printing Office, 1876). 89 pp.

with the history of the country concerned, whereas all other biography (with the exception of a limited number of special groups
which are scattered throughout the tables) is classed in the 920's.
Most libraries today ignore the subdivisions of the 920 class.

The association of geography with history derives from the fact
that the early concepts of both geography and history were primarily
political. Since Montesquieu's attempt to show that political institutions are conditioned by geographic factors, the two disciplines had
been closely related. Furthermore, early accounts of travellers
and explorers provided much of the data for both geographers and
historians; Montesquieu himself had attempted to draw scientific
generalizations from these unscientific and frequently inaccurate
narratives. Even today these early accounts often provide the only
available data for the social history of their respective regions.
Thus the 910 class will contain much material of interest to the
sociologist, the anthropologist, and even the geologist, as well as
to the historian. But because of the great popularity of travel books
among general readers most of the books to be found in the 910's
are popular contemporary treatments such as those of Richard
Halliburton and Lowell Thomas, which are useful only as recreational
reading. The classification system provides no mechanism for sep-
arating the trivial from the substantial or the scholarly.

The End of the Nineteenth Century

The outstanding influences in American historiography during
the latter half of the nineteenth century were those of the German
seminar and the work of Leopold von Ranke. Henry Adams, who
studied in Germany, brought to Harvard the seminar method of instruction and set his students to work "burrowing like rabbits all
over the historical terrain". By many, Adams is regarded as the
only truly philosophical historian that America has ever produced.
Certainly he is a fascinating figure whose life was a failure only
in his inability to adjust to an age in which he felt himself essentially
a stranger. An eighteenth century spirit with a twentieth century
mind, he was unable to find happiness in an industrial society wherein the intellect played a relatively minor role. Disgusted and dis-
illusioned with public life he turned to historical investigation as
an escape from an environment in which he regarded himself as a
complete failure. His Life of Albert Gallatin is still unsurpassed,
and his nine-volume History of the United States during the administration of Jefferson and Madison is in every sense a great work
that may be still read with profit by both layman and scholar.
Though the work was primarily political in treatment, the intro-
ductory chapters of the first volume and the concluding chapters of
the ninth remain one of the best treatments of American social
history. The last American aristocrat in the eighteenth century
sense, he viewed history from an Olympian height, that put to shame

72

the babblings of his predecessors.

But despite this conspicuous success, he regarded his work as essentially a failure, escaped to the South Seas where he discovered a new appreciation of beauty and for a time became engrossed in aesthetics. A visit to the Chicago World's Fair of 1893 promoted an interest in the dynamo (force) and he became involved in a search for dynamic principles that would explain historical movements. He saw in the development of world history the operation of five stages of force: (a) the force of animal desire, in the prehistoric era; (b) the force of faith, operating predominantly to 1600 A. D.; (c) the force of mechanical energy, 1600-1900 A. D.; (d) the force of electricity, in the early twentieth century; and (e) the force of radium in the coming era. Derived from the Second Law of Thermo-dynamics, this philosophy saw the exhaustion of force as the underlying law of historical evolution. Each age endured for a length of time equal to the square root of the preceding era. As force was accelerated thought was accelerated, and as thought was accelerated action was accelerated, thus energy was expended until all energy was exhausted. Such a philosophy was obviously a reaction against the evolutionary theory, but it still demonstrated the possibilities inherent in a scientific approach to historical phenomena.

John Fiske stands in direct opposition to Henry Adams. Beginning as a philosopher and ending as a historian, his work represents a complete surrender to the doctrine of evolution. Possessor of a brilliant mind that mastered many languages, he travelled in Europe where he was greatly influenced by the work of Comte, Huxley, and Darwin. His genius was for popularization rather than for creative historical research. His Discovery of America and his Critical Period are his most important works, though both have been largely superseded today.

The influence of German scholarship, especially the writings of von Ranke, and the introduction of the German seminar reached fruition in the work of Herbert B. Adams. Henry Adams brought the German seminar method of instruction to Harvard, and C. K. Adams introduced it at the University of Michigan, but it was Herbert B. Adams who is, probably, best known for its extensive use in graduate teaching and research. Although his own theory, the "primordial Germ School" is no longer taken seriously, he became at Johns Hopkins a teacher of tremendous influence and prestige, whose class rolls read almost like a who's who of American historians. Woodrow Wilson, Frederick Jackson Turner, John R. Commons, John Dewey, John Spencer Bassett, Richard T. Ely, and Thorstein Veblen are but a few of the distinguished names listed among his students. Thus, by the end of the century American historical scholarship was beginning to enter a new phase; comprehensive history was on the decline, and the seminar had encouraged the minute investigation of specific and restricted problems. This change was reflected in the proliferation of journals, a form more appropriate than the book for the publication of the results of such research.

There were two important consequences of these changes in historical scholarship: (a) much of the best historical research was no longer presented in a style or through media which would attract readers among the general public; and (b) new problems arose in making such publications known and accessible to historical scholars. Organized efforts to ensure continuing bibliographic services in history began in the United States during this period. Probably many American historians were familiar with the German Jahreberichte der Geschichts-wissenschaft im Auftrage der Historischen Gesellschaft zu Berlin herausgegeben (1878-1913) and the Bibliographie zur deutschen Geschichte (1888-1927) and had these in mind as models during the early struggles of the American Historical Association to promote the publication of adequate bibliographies of American history. With the aid of a federal subsidy for printing the Association has sponsored the best continuing bibliography:

> Griffin, Grace Gardner, comp. Writings on American History, 1906- A bibliography of books and articles ... Washington: Govt. print. off., 1908-

The Association also sponsored the standard bibliography of general history, now somewhat out of date:

> A Guide to Historical Literature; ed. by G. M. Dutcher, H. R. Shipman, S. B. Fay, A. H. Shere, W. H. Allison. N. Y.: Macmillan, 1937. 1222 pp.

and the more specialized:

> Bemis, Samuel Flagg and Griffin, Grace Gardner. Guide to the Diplomatic History of the United States, 1775-1921. ... Washington: U. S. Govt. print. off., 1935. 979 pp.

The best bibliography of bibliographies in American history is:

> Beers, Henry Putney. Bibliographies in American History: Guide to Materials for Research. Rev. ed. N. Y.: Wilson, 1942. 487 pp.

A notable cooperative enterprise in international bibliography is:

> International Bibliography of Historical Sciences. Internationale bibliographie der geschichtswissenschaften. International bibliografia de las ciencias historicas. Bibliographie internationale des sciences historiques. Bibliografia internazionale delle scienze storiche. 1926- N. Y.: Wilson, 1930- v. 1-

Regionalism

Frederick Jackson Turner's great contribution to American historical writing lay in his gift to American historiography of a completely new and unique orientation that made it something more than a . slavish following of European schools of thought. Partly because he was an inspiring teacher and partly because of the importance of his interpretation he has achieved a wider influence than any other historian of recent years, even to the extent that his ideas have been defended, expanded, and modified by his disciples to the point at which it has become difficult to rediscover with exactness his own point of view. Yet the bulk of his writings is not large; most of his work appeared in essays and monographs and one might say of him that probably no one in American historical writing has achieved such great influence with so relatively little publication.

In a literal sense Turner was not a regionalist, since his primary concern was with a process rather than with a geographic section of the American continent. But two types of regional development in American historiography opened the way for Turner's work -- (a) the writings of historians like Parkman, Herbert Howe Bancroft, and later Theodore Roosevelt, all of whom were concerned with the West as a historical entity, and (b) the collection of historical documents relating to the West such as the Draper collection at the University of Wisconsin. Furthermore, as early as 1824 Jefferson achieved an amazingly close approximation of Turner's wave theory, and Emerson, Macaulay, and Lord Bryce had all emphasized the influence of the frontier upon the course of American history.

Turner's basic theme was that American history to 1893 was in large measure a story of Western colonization, and that the existence of free land and the continuous advance of settlement largely explained the uniqueness of American social and political institutions. The great creative force in American life and the shaping influence upon its social and economic patterns was generated by this expansion. There was not just a single frontier, but a series of successive frontiers, or waves, that moved westward, each carrying with it its own particular characteristics or influences, a "cutting edge" of civilization that shaped the life, not only of the West but of the East from whence it had come. Much of American history, then, is largely to be interpreted in terms of conflict between regions or sections, and in this struggle the frontier acted as a safety-valve offering a release for those in the East who, for lack of opportunity at home, might look to the West with hope. The frontier was a laboratory in which social institutions might be tested; it promoted democracy, individualism, and nationalism; and it was the great source of American prosperity. Now that the West is settled, the nation must find other means for the stimulation of those opportunities and advantages which, to 1893, were natural phenomena.

Turner was thus the first in America to examine minutely the real influence of geography upon history, and to perceive the relationship between geographical environment and political ideas. He was the first to draw heavily upon the findings of the other social

sciences to support and illuminate historical investigation, the first
to write "social history" as it is understood today. He may be criticized for his excessive emphasis on the democratic influence of the
frontier, his failure to perceive that the frontier often degraded rather
than improved the status of the frontiersman, his neglect of such important factors as urbanization, class conflict, or the aping of the
East by the West, but at least he and his followers elevated the study
of "local" history to a point where it could make a substantial contribution to the study of national growth. Directly or indirectly the
foundation had been laid for the work of such historians as William
A. Dunning, Ulrich B. Phillips, and William E. Dodd.

The New History

The advent of the "New History" had already been foreshadowed
in the earlier attempts to make history a "science", and to broaden
its scope. The work of the graduate schools in training for historical
scholarship had been most successful in eliminating the many inac-
curacies of older historical interpretations, but at the same time the
new approach had largely killed history as "literature," substituting
the compact monograph for the broad philosophical treatment, stressing
information and analysis rather than synthesis, and creating a blind
and unreasoning worship of footnotes and citations. In short, they
had made great strides in advancing the scholarly accuracy of historical research, but in so doing had destroyed much of the popularity that historical writing had enjoyed during the preceding century.
At the same time there began to be published a number of scholarly
journals, with an audience largely limited to professional historians,
which supplied an outlet for the dissemination of the short monographic
treatments characteristic of the new history. Even had these been
written in a manner that would have made them appetizing to the popular reader their contents would not have been accessible to the general public to the extent that the volumes of Bancroft, Prescott, and
Parkman had been.
The coming of the "New History" brought with it an initial reaction against the heavy academic approach that had been the contribution
of the German seminar. It sought to extend the scope of history by
adapting the methods and findings of other social disciplines, economics, political science, psychology, and the like. The rise of indus-
trialization and urbanization tended to discredit the "great man" theory of history and give increasing attention to men in the mass. The
"common man" became important to a degree that he had never before
enjoyed. The von Rankean conception of absolute truth in history was
discredited, and bias, in the sense of point of view, was taken for
granted. Finally, there emerged a new emphasis upon synthesis in
historical writing, a horizontal synthesis that endeavored to present
the entire complex of social, economic, and political forces that constituted the entirety of the historical pattern.

There is no doubt that the "New History" contributed much to the enrichment of historical writing and the deepening of our understanding of the past. Especially is this true of the work of James Harvey Robinson, the earlier work of Charles A. Beard, and the historical presentation typified by the History of American Life series. But like all movements, it has its own peculiar weaknesses and excesses. The service rendered by Robinson, and his disciple Harry Elmer Barnes, in integrating history with the other social sciences has been very great indeed, but at times it has led to an eagerness to display a familiarity with sociological terminology without a real understanding of this new vocabulary. Furthermore, the belief that history should frankly abandon a striving for objectivity and seek to present always the liberal or progressive point of view is a potentially dangerous tendency, even when one finds himself in agreement with the point of view expressed. The emphasis on the "common man" may well lead to a corresponding neglect of the "uncommon man" who, after all, really did play a significant role in the shaping of historical events. History that "follows the headlines" may quite easily fail to penetrate sufficiently below the surface of social history to divulge the entirety of social forces that determine the historical pattern. Excessive emphasis on contemporary history has led to the neglect of older periods which stand in need of re-examination and which might well be studied with profit. In summary, this concern with contemporary events has decreased perspective, intensified the element of bias, increased the conviction that history should defend a particular social point of view, and in general tended to discredit most historical writing before 1920.

The Writing of History at Mid-Century

The aftermath of the second World War brought with it a demand for the reinterpretation of American history parallel to that which occurred during the generation that followed the European conflict of 1914 to 1918. Historians of this earlier period had rallied about either Wilsonian idealism or the popular pessimism of Spengler and Henry Adams. The new doctrine of relativism brought with it a new sense of emancipation, and the "debunkers" set to work to loosen the foundations of established reputations and traditional interpretations. From their attacks no national hero or established institution was secure. Ardent pacifists rewrote history to prove that war was futile, that diplomats were worse than incompetent, and that America had been drawn into a European conflict by the interventionists for the sake of salvaging American investment abroad.

The signing of the peace treaties with Germany and Japan brought to the cloistered world of the professional historians another period of turmoil and academic dissension. In 1946 the Committee on Historiography of the Social Science Research Council published a collection of essays entitled The Theory and Practice of Historical

Study. This volume, though it actually added little to the historical theory of the 1920's, drew much public attention to the alleged malaise that was assumed to be characteristic of historical scholarship.

The innumerable conferences, special investigations, and inconclusive experiments that followed eventually proved only that there was to be no "New History" in any revolutionary sense. That though the historians might well make use of the "scientific" methods presented to them by the other social sciences, they were to remain historians in their own right. As Professor Woodward has stated the case:

> The great majority of historians, I think, quietly decided that they were neither scientists nor literary artists but historians -- sui generis and without apology. They might consider becoming companions of the social sciences, but never their handmaids. They would maintain a healthy concern with the present without losing their dedication to the reality of the past. They would read the anthropologists and sociologists but would continue to write the best English they could. And above all they would never invent a private language. [11]

This last was doubtless prompted by the increasingly heavy competition that the academic historian has had to face from the competent amateur. The very substantial work of such lay scholars as Carl Sandburg, Douglas S. Freeman, Robert E. Sherwood, Bernard DeVoto, Margaret Leech, and Esther Forbes has not only elevated the standards of historical scholarship but has also revived its literary significance. In the wake of this wholesome influence has come a rebirth of historical writing for popular consumption that is reminiscent of the age of Bancroft, Parkman, and Prescott. There have been no debunkers in the present postwar generation. The popularity of such titles as Robert E. Lee, Lee's Lieutenants, Reveille in Washington, Paul Revere, and Roosevelt and Hopkins, are symptomatic of the desire of the public to gain a really objective understanding of the American past and the figures that lived in it.

Monumental and really important biographies have been pouring from the presses in astonishing numbers. Most of the Virginia Dynasty of Presidents have been subjected to such exhaustive treatment. Three generations of the Adams family have received biographical attention, and Henry Adams alone has been the subject of no less than five biographies published since the war. There have been two biographies of Calhoun, and Lincoln has been the subject of several impressive and enduring works.

The integration of political and intellectual history, begun in such

---

[11]
C. Vann Woodward. "Report on Current Research: American History" Saturday Review, April 4, 1953. p. 16 ff.

monumental studies as those of Beard and Vernon L. Parrington, has been continued in the writings of Richard Hofstadter, Arthur M. Schlesinger, Jr., Merle Curti, and Ralph H. Gabriel. The trend toward emphasis on intellectual and cultural history has been reflected in the establishment at many universities of departments or committees on American Civilization, and similar inter-disciplinary area study groups, a development which has, in large measure, superseded the traditional "schools of thought" that characterized the historical scholarship of a previous generation. Such an integrated and cooperative attack by scholars upon subject fields in which the cross-fertilization of ideas and points-of-view is so rewarding, has very important implications for the present structure of our bibliographic system, as well as for the library organization of the future. No longer can the historian remain ignorant of the work of his colleagues in contiguous fields, and no longer do the records of scholarship admit of classification into discrete and independent compartments with fixed and clearly definable boundaries. Adaptability, flexibility, responsiveness to change, these will become increasingly important criteria by which the effectiveness of future bibliographic services and systems and the procedures of the librarian will be judged.

This inter-disciplinary attack upon historical problems has materially enriched the success of inquiries into a variety of specialized areas of investigation. The significant work of Carl Wittke, Oscar Handlin, and Theodore C. Blegen on the influence of the immigrant in American life has made important additions to sociological as well as to historical knowledge. The economic historians have been busily investigating the annals of business enterprise, with the result that several monumental histories of large business firms are well under way.

A revival of interest in military history has been at least encouraged, if not actually initiated, by the activities of the armed forces in making the records of their operations during the Second World War available to competent historians. In many instances governmental subsidy has been provided for the publication of extensive multi-volume histories of military, naval and aeronautical operations. There has been some revival of interest in the Revolution and the War of 1812, but the greatest of activities, especially among lay groups, have been those of local organizations which have convened at frequent intervals to recount the battles of the War Between the States, or to relive the exploits of Custer and his contemporaries in their last forays against the vanishing Redman.

The history of American transportation, especially of the railroad and the automobile, and their impact upon our social and economic life, has increasingly attracted the attention of scholar and layman alike. The so-called "Lexington Group," for the promotion of historical investigation into the American railroad, has been one of the most active sections of the Mississippi Valley Historical Association. Similarly, concern with the historical development of medicine has occupied many competent scholars, and one might go on and on with parallel investigation into American folk music, art, education, libraries, and the various media of popular entertainment, sports, and other forms of recreation. The origins of baseball, for example, has recently aroused considerable interest beyond that of the professional sports-writer.

Summary and synthesis may generally be regarded as signifying the end, rather than the beginning, of a creative period. There is, indeed, some evidence that the inquiries of the past half-century have necessitated new syntheses and reevaluations. A number of such comprehensive undertakings are at present either under way or are being planned. Allan Nevins has undertaken a one-man synthesis of the mid-nineteenth century sectional conflict comparable to the earlier work of Rhodes. Henry Steele Commanger has enlisted a considerable group of writers for the preparation of a multi-volume review of the entirety of American history. Wendell Stevenson and E. Merton Coulter are editing a ten volume history of the South.

Finally, one may legitimately surmise that this country is on the verge of a new era of intense nationalism, which would doubtless stimulate increasing interest in the origin and development of American institutions, though it might not necessarily promote the soundness or objectivity of our scholarship.

Bibliography

American Historiography - Colonial Period

Smith, John. The Generall Historie of Virginia, New England & the Summer Isles. ... Glasgow: J. MacLehose and Sons, 1907. 2 v.

Bradford, William. History of Plymouth Plantation 1620-1647 ... Boston: Massachusetts Historical Society, 1912.

Winthrop, John. ... (Winthrop's)Journal, "History of New England," 1630-1649, ed. by James Kendall Hosmer. New York: Scribner, 1908.

Mather, Increase. A Brief History of the War with the Indians in New England From June 24, 1675 ... to August 12, 1676 ... London: Printed for Richard Chiswell, 1676. University Microfilms. Amer. Culture Series no. 75 (Roll 7) Original in the William L. Clements Library.

_____. Remarkable Providences Illustrative of the Earlier Days of American Colonization ... London: Reeves and Turner, 1890.

Mather, Cotton. Magnalia Christi Americana: or, The Ecclesiastical History of New England. Hartford: S. Andrews and Son, 1853-55.

_____. Diary of Cotton Mather. Boston: Massachusetts Historical Society, 1911-12. (Half-title -- Collections of the Massachusetts Historical Society, ser. 7, v. 7-8)

Franklin, Benjamin. Benjamin Franklin's Autobiographical Writings, selected and edited by Carl Van Doren. New York: The Viking Press, 1945.

Crevecoeur, Michel Guillaume St. Jean de, called St. Jean Crevecoeur. Letters from an American Farmer. London: Dent; New York: Dutton; (1912) (Half-title -- Everyman's Library, ed. by Ernest Rhys. Travel and Biography)

Sewall, Samuel. Diary, 1674-1729. Boston: Massachusetts Historical Society, 1878-82. (Collections of the Massachusetts Historical Society, ser. 5, v. 5-7)

Stith, William. The History of the First Discovery and Settlement of Virginia ... New York: J. Sabin, 1865.

Prince, Thomas. A Chronological History of New England, in the Form of Annals ... Boston: Cummings, Hilliard and Company, 1826.

Hutchinson, Thomas. The History of the Colony and Province of Massachusetts Bay. Cambridge: Harvard University Press, 1936.

The Period of the Republic, 1776-1820

Marshall, John. The Life of George Washington. Philadelphia: J. Crissy, etc., 1839.

Weems, Mason Clocke. The Life of George Washington. Philadelphia. J. B. Lippincott, 1867.

Trumbull, Benjamin. A Complete History of Connecticut ... New London: H. D. Otley, 1898. 2 v.

Burk, John Daly. History of Virginia ... Petersburg, Va.: Dickson and Pescud, 1804-1816. 4 v.

Belknap, Jeremy. The History of New Hampshire ... Dover, N. H.: S. C. Stevens and Ela S. Wadleigh, 1831.

_____. American Biography ... New York: Harper, 1855.

Mid-Nineteenth Century American Histories

Bancroft, George. History of the United States of America, from the Discovery of the Continent. New York: Appleton and Company, 1891-93. (Closes with 1789)

Hildreth, Richard. The History of the United States of America. New York: Harper and Brothers, c. 1877-80.

Prescott, William Hickling. History of the Conquest of Mexico, and History of the Conquest of Peru. New York: The Modern Library, (1936)

Parkman, Francis. Montcalm and Wolfe. France and England in North America ... Boston: Little,Brown and Company, 1924.

The End of the Nineteenth Century

Adams, Henry. History of the United States of America ... New York: A. and C. Boni, 1930. 9 v. in 4.

Fiske, John. The Critical Period of American History, 1783-1789 ... Boston and New York: Houghton Mifflin Company, c. 1916.

Adams, Herbert B. Historical Scholarship in the United States, 1876-1901; As Revealed in the Correspondence of Herbert B. Adams; ed. by W. Hull Holt ... Baltimore: Johns Hopkins Press, 1938. (The Johns Hopkins University Studies in Historical and Political Science)

Regionalism

Turner, Frederick Jackson. The Frontier in American History. New York: Holt and Company, 1921.

_____. The Early Writings of Frederick Jackson Turner; With a List of All His Works, compiled by Everett E. Edwards. Madison: The University of Wisconsin Press, 1938. (To be noted as an example of bio-bibliography)

Phillips, Ulrich Bonnell. Life and Labor in the Old South. Boston: Little, Brown and Company, 1929.

The New History

Robinson, James Harvey. The New History; Essays Illustrating the Modern Historical Outlook. New York: Macmillan, 1912.

Barnes, Harry Elmer. A Survey of Western Civilization. New York:
T. Y. Crowell Company, 1947.

History of American Life (series) ed. by Arthur M. Schlesinger and
Dixon Ryan Fox. New York: Macmillan Company, 1927-50.
13 v. A few of the titles in this series are:
Adams, James Truslow. The Coming of the White Man
Green, Everts B. The Revolutionary Generation
Fish, Carl R. The Rise of the Common Man
Cole, Arthur C. The Irrepressible Conflict
Nevins, Allan. The Emergence of Modern America
Tarbell, Ida M. The Nationalizing of Business
Schlesinger, Arthur M. The Rise of the City
Wecter, Dixon. The Age of the Great Depression

Mid-Twentieth Century

De Voto, Bernard. The Year of Decision. Boston: Little, Brown,
1943.

_____. Across the Wide Missouri. Boston: Houghton Mifflin, 1947.

_____. The Course of Empire. Boston: Houghton Mifflin, 1952.

Forbes, Esther. Paul Revere and the World he Lived in. Boston:
Houghton Mifflin, 1942.

Freeman, Douglas S. Robert E. Lee. N. Y.: Scribner, 1934. 4 v.

_____. Lee's Lieutenants. N. Y.: Scribner, 1942-44. 3 v.

Sandburg, Carl. Abraham Lincoln: the Prairie Years. N. Y.:
Harcourt, 1920. 2 v.

_____. Abraham Lincoln: The War Years. N. Y.: Harcourt, 1939.
4 v.

Freeman, Douglas S. George Washington; a Biography. N. Y.:
Scribner, 1948-

Malone, Dumas. Jefferson and his Time. Boston: Little, Brown.
1948-

Bemis, Samuel F. John Quincy Adams and the Foundations of American
Foreign Policy. N. Y.: Knopf, 1949.

Lipsky, George A. John Quincy Adams, his Theory and Ideas. N. Y.:
Crowell, 1950.

Randall, James G. Lincoln -- the President. N. Y.: Dodd Mead, 1948-52. 3 v.

Colt, Margaret I. John C. Calhoun, American Portrait. Boston: Houghton Mifflin, 1950.

Samuels, Ernest. The Young Henry Adams. Cambridge: Harvard University Press, 1948.

Curti, Merle. The Growth of American Thought. N. Y.: Harper, 1943.

Handlin, Oscar C. This Was America. Cambridge: Harvard University Press, 1949.

_____. The Uprooted. Boston: Little, Brown, 1951.

Wittke, Carl F. We who Built America. Cleveland, Ohio: Western Reserve University Press, 1950.

Emmet, Boris and Jeuck, John E. Catalogues and Counters, a History of Sears Roebuck and Company. Chicago: University of Chicago Press, 1950.

CHAPTER V

SOCIAL AND INTELLECTUAL ORGANIZATION OF THE WORK OF THE

HISTORIAN

The development of historical scholarship, like that of other disciplines, follows a characteristic pattern which begins with the work
of isolated individuals. During this period of fragmentation, each
scholar investigates problems entirely of his own choosing, in his
own way, and by means of methods and techniques hammered out
as best he can from the resources immediately available to him.
As the discipline matures, and the body of accumulated knowledge in-
creases in bulk and complexity, the scholar discovers that it is no
longer necessary or desirable for him to pursue an isolated course.
Thus the various forms of communication among scholars begin to
emerge, first as direct personal communication and later, in the more
elaborate forms of institutionalization through the founding of historical associations, the establishment of educational agencies for the
training of scholars, and eventually the action of government itself
in encouraging the pursuit of historical investigation as a guide to
political and social policy.

At the same time that this process of institutionalization is developing a formalized structure, and as a consequence of improved communication among scholars, standardized techniques and methods of
work are crystallized. Though these methods vary in detail from
scholar to scholar and from subject to subject depending upon the nature of the problems, the materials available, and the point of view
represented, nevertheless it becomes possible to describe a model
pattern of work characteristic of historical research generally -- a
kind of "ideal type" of historian at work. Such a pattern of operation,
in its turn, influences the form of organization of materials needed
by the scholar: the creation of libraries, both as repositories and
agencies for the systematization of bibliographic resources; the publication of "corpora" of source documents; and the compilation of
bibliographic materials that will bring to the scholar the resources
he requires in a form most useful to him.

But the scholar not only needs access to the source materials of
history, he must also acquaint himself with the methodology applicable to his craft, even though such methods may have been developed
from without the historical discipline by investigators in other fields.
Though much has been written about the historical method, there
exists no standard basic guide to the bibliography of historical meth-

odology in the other social sciences, such as Dorothy Culver's
Methodology of Social Science Research; a Bibliography, [1] but for the
most part he goes directly to the titles with which he is already familiar or which are brought to his attention by reviews in the journals
he regularly peruses, such as:

American Historical Review
English Historical Review
Journal of Modern History
Mississippi Valley Historical Review
Journal of Negro History
etc.

The librarian is interested in organization of patterns of work
at both the individual and the societal level for both forms affect his
own institution and his own operations within that institution.

Institutionalization

Institutionalization in any field creates the necessary machinery
both to stimulate and to implement the forces of supply and demand
which increase the volume of publication, influence the forms of publication, and establish patterns of organization which will be imposed,
with some modifications, upon educational systems, museums, and
libraries. In the field of history this institutionalization has mani-
fested itself in the United States[2] through (1) the establishment of academic chairs and departments of history; (2) the founding of historical
societies of two kinds, the local historical groups composed of interested amateurs, and later the professional historical societies, notably the American Historical Association; (3) the support of libraries
and musuems, frequently by the local historical groups; and (4) the
participation of the federal government in promoting and subsidizing
the writing and publication of historical materials.

In the academic curriculum history began as a secondary interest
associated with theology, the classics, the study of other foreign languages, geography, and antiquities. In part its origins are to be
found in literary history where it emerged from the chronicle, the
narrative of adventure, and other manifestations of the universal
impulse to keep a record of important events.

As early as 1643 Harvard offered a course in history during the
winter term, and in 1722 the Hollis chair of divinity, which included

---

[1]
Dorothy C. Culver. Methodology of Social Science Research; a
Bibliography. (Berkeley: Univ. of California Press, 1936). 159 pp.

[2]
Parallel developments might well be traced in other countries,
but limitations of space prevent a fuller treatment here.

the teaching of church history and Jewish antiquities, was established
at the same institution. American history was being taught by the
Rev. William Stith at William and Mary in 1731. King's College offered a course in "geography and history" in 1754, and seven years
later the College of New Jersey, now Princeton, offered a course in
"geography and chronology." At Columbia the Rev. John Gross
offered a comprehensive course in history (based largely on geography)
during the years from 1784 to 1795.

Not until after 1800 did history dissociate itself from other academic disciplines and assume separate status. After 1825 instruction
in history appeared with increasing frequency in college curricula,
modern rather than ancient history being the first to achieve independence. The growing spirit of American nationalism encouraged emphasis on American history, but though it had been taught at William
and Mary as early as 1731, other colleges did not introduce it into
their courses of study until after the beginning of the nineteenth century. The first separate chair of history was founded at Harvard in
1839, with Jared Sparks, who was primarily interested in modern history and particularly American history, as professor. These tendencies were given further emphasis by the teaching of Thomas R. Dew
at William and Mary and of Francis Lieber, at South Carolina College
and later at Columbia. Lieber is especially important not only because he is considered to be one of the greatest scholars in the social
sciences in America before 1865, but also because of his interest in
promoting historical interpretation as a guide to social understanding.

Formal instruction in history was hampered by the absence of
adequate translations and textbooks prepared for classroom use.
Jefferson, in outlining a course of readings in modern history, was
compelled to rely almost entirely upon such voluminous standard
works as those of Hume, Robertson, Gibbon, Hallam, and Voltaire.
The Bohn translations, which at the time of their publication were the
best sources for classical and modern works, did not begin to appear
until well after 1800. Not until the second quarter of the nineteenth
century were there available textbooks especially prepared for and
adapted to college instruction in history.

From the period that followed the Civil War to the end of the nineteenth century, the teaching of history, like that of the other social
sciences, underwent profound changes. As has already been shown,
the influence of the German historians was remarkably strong and the
development of the spirit and content of scientific inquiry was very
great. Similarly, formal instruction in history evinced a concurrent
growth. In 1884 there were about twenty men of professorial rank
teaching history in American colleges, but by 1895 this number had
increased to approximately one hundred, about half of whom had
studied at German universities. Although history became well established during the nineteenth century as a separate department of
academic instruction, its central emphasis was still so predominantly
political that the history of special subjects, such as economics,
sociology, political science, philosophy, etc., was left to those de-

partments, a segregation which, as we have seen, was reflected in the library classification schemes devised during this period. Librarians were merely reflecting the belief commonly held among scholars that the boundaries among the academic disciplines were fixed in a stable and comprehensive pattern which might serve as a universal and permanent basis for the organization of the resulting literature.

But with the opening of the twentieth century there came a new trend toward synthesis among the academic disciplines generally, culminating by the middle of the present century in the general education movement, which tends to break down all disciplinary barriers and to focus upon major problem areas all knowledge available from any source.

The teaching of history in the elementary and high schools has followed a path parallel to that of instruction at the college level. Here, too, history emerged as an auxiliary to other subjects of study -- geography, the classics, Biblical history. Not until after 1830 did history acquire an independent place in the elementary school program. Though in 1827 some fifteen textbooks in the subject had been published in this country, as late as 1860 only a small proportion of the pupils in the elementary schools of the country were studying the subject. In that year only 1.35 per cent of the pupils in the common schools of Ohio, which is probably typical of the country as a whole, were pursuing history as a subject of study. Toward the end of the nineteenth century the work of Johann Friedrich Herbart, of the University of Koenigsberg, began to exercise a strong influence upon elementary education in this country. It was Herbart's belief that education should develop personal character and prepare the individual for social usefulness, and history was held to be the most effective subject to achieve these objectives. Thus, through the influence of the Herbartians, history began to assume an important place in the curriculum of the elementary grades. This tendency was given further impetus by the work in 1893 and 1895 of the National Educational Association, and in 1899 and 1908 by the American Historical Association. By 1900, history, other than American, was being taught to 38 per cent of the high school students in the United States, and ten years later over 90 per cent offered instruction in ancient history, 43 per cent offered English history, and about 70 per cent of the schools required American history as a pre-requisite to graduation.

By 1920 the elementary grades, and somewhat later the high schools, began to break away from the traditional methods of teaching history as a chronological sequence of national heroes and dramatic episodes, and inter-disciplinary topics had begun to be emphasized. This lessening of emphasis upon formal history, as taught at the beginning of the century, brought with it greater attention to general social problems, and increased awareness of the historical importance of inventions, commerce, agriculture, and especially of current events.

Concurrently with the multiplication of academic chairs and departments of history and the increase in the number of full-time teaching personnel at both the college and secondary school levels, arose the first of the really professional historical associations, of which the most important is the American Historical Association, established in 1884, with a membership now close to four thousand. This organization is composed largely of teachers of history in American universities, colleges, and secondary schools. By contrast, the Mississippi Valley Historical Association, established in 1907, in spite of the regionalism implicit in its title, is primarily an organization of teachers of American history, and its scope is increasingly expanding to include the entire field of research in American history.

For the librarian the American Historical Association is particularly important because of its leadership in bibliographic activity in the historical disciplines. As early as 1889, five years after its founding, the Association published, as part of its annual report, A Partial Bibliography of the Published Works of Members of the American Historical Association, prepared by Paul Leicester Ford. Later, as Part II of its annual report for 1905, appeared the fourth edition of the Bibliography of Historical Societies of the United States and British America, which is still a valuable research tool, as it is the only key to materials of this kind. In it are listed the published proceedings of all important historical societies, from their dates of founding, the earliest of which goes back to 1792. These publications include a large part of the scholarly historical writing of the period and many accounts of primary source materials of which no other description is available.

Several important special bibliographies, compiled by individuals, were published during the early years as parts of its annual reports, but as early as 1895 the Association began to work through committees definitely charged with responsibility for planning and promoting systematic bibliographic enterprises. In the preceding year A. Howard Clark, in an article on "The United States Government in History,"[3] wrote: "The time may be ripe, too, for this association to prepare a complete, classified, and fully indexed analytical bibliography of all works in manuscript or print, in English or in foreign tongues, that concern the history of this great nation." In 1895, the Committee on Bibliography established a working relationship with the American Library Association for the promotion of coordinated bibliography in history. The publication by the American Library Association of Joseph N. Larned's The Literature of American History: a Bibliographical Guide was one of the most import tangible results of this early cooperation. Finally, one should mention the very important annual Writings on American History, 1906, compiled for many years by Grace Gardner Griffin and which, after passing from one publisher to another, was established as a regular publication of the Government Printing Office.[4]

3

Annual Report of the Association, 1894, p. 554.

4

Summarized from Robert Rosenthal: Thesis in progress on the bibliographic activities of the American Historical Association.

State and local historical societies have flourished in the United
States for more than a century and a half. The first state association,
that of Massachusetts, was established in 1791 under the leadership
of Jeremy Belknap. Today more than nine hundred such organizations
are in existence. At its second meeting the Massachusetts Historical
Society founded a library which in five years contained one thousand
volumes, exclusive of pamphlets, newspapers and manuscripts, and
by 1859 the collection numbered fourteen thousand volumes. Other
of the more important early societies with important historical library collections were the New York Historical Society, the American
Antiquarian Society, and the Essex Historical Society. Though most
of the local societies have been energetic in collecting historical materials, relatively few have been successful in building libraries of more
than local importance. Together with libraries, most of the societies
have made some attempt to establish museums ranging from the ubiquitous
cabinet of Indian arrow-heads to general collections of really significant
artifacts. The major historical societies all support substantial publication programs, many of which are of considerable scholarly value.
Most of this material is inaccessible except through special bibliographies, inasmuch as few libraries analyze such series. There are
two useful guides to the local historical societies:

Dunlap, Leslie W. American Historical Societies, 1790-1860.
Madison, Wisconsin; Privately Printed, 1944. 238 p.

American Association for State and Local Society. Historical
Societies in the United States and Canada; A Handbook. Washington,
D. C.: The Association, 1944. 261 pp.

Assumption by the government of responsibility for the collection
and publication of important public documents has previously been
mentioned. As examples one might cite the publication of the voluminous series of official records of the War of the Rebellion, and the
contribution made by the Department of State and later by the National
Archives in publishing the territorial papers of the United States.
Similarly, subsidization of the publishing activities of the American
Historical Association by the federal government had undoubtedly made
possible an extension of the bibliographic work of that association.
The Library of Congress, through its sponsorship of Bemis and Griffin's
important Guide to the Diplomatic History of the United States has made
a lasting contribution to the bibliography of American history. Today
the federal government has taken an active part in encouraging the
publication of official histories of certain of its agencies, and especially
of its military, naval, and air force operations during the second
World War.[5]

---

[5]
A detailed treatment of the institutional development of the library
is presented in a paper, "Emergence of a New Institutional Structure for
the Dissemination of Specialized Information" read by the author before
the conference on "The Communication of Specialized Information" sponsored by the Graduate Library School of the University of Chicago in August 195?

Analysis of the Typical Work Pattern of the Historian

Seldom does the historian choose his subject completely and entirely of his own volition. One might even go so far as to say that more often the subject chooses him, at least to the extent that it develops either logically or fortuitously from his environment -- the suggestion of a colleague, the product of his reading, the pressure of an immediate social problem, the impact of circumstance. But once the problem has been defined, and its constituent elements analyzed, the exercise of volition plays an increasingly important role. But even here the selection of a point of view, the determination of an approach, and the analysis of the interpretation are conditioned by his own previous experience, the climate of opinion within which he works, and the materials available to him.

At this point he will begin to search the literature to discover the extent to which the subject has been treated by others, and if so the degree to which his approach differs from theirs. For this purpose he will have recourse to the appropriate historical bibliographies, including lists of doctoral dissertations. Having satisfied himself that his problem merits investigation he may find it necessary to extend his auxiliary reading to strengthen his grasp of all the factors to which his problem is related. Such investigation is not confined to history in the strict sense, but extends to any of the other branches of knowledge which may contribute hypotheses, methods, or substantive knowledge to the exploration of his immediate problem. For guidance in such less familiar subject areas he is likely to apply to the librarian for assistance in locating the best bibliographies of the appropriate related or auxiliary sciences; and as he is likely to be unfamiliar with this literature his most useful aids will be highly selective bibliographies, preferably annotated, compiled by scholars of acknowledged authority. The use of abstracting services, if any exist, will be most economical of his time and yet productive of the most valuable results.

Having fortified his position with this exploratory reading he may proceed with the formulation of his hypothesis or hypotheses and with the selection of methods most certain to provide an adequate test of his major hypothesis. This determination of hypothesis and method almost automatically suggests the types of evidence relevant to his investigation. But this universe of potential evidence must then be narrowed to a more limited range of the major types most highly significant for his purpose and practicably available to him with a reasonable expenditure of time, effort, and money. Although this part of the procedure is largely an intellectual rather than a strictly bibliographic operation, the librarian must have a thorough understanding of it, not only for its relevance to any historical investigation in librarianship which he himself may wish to undertake, but also in order to give intelligent assistance to those innumerable students who come to him asking for "all the material about my thesis topic." Such an inquiry should never be answered by providing one or more relevant bibliographies or by the hasty or arbitrary selection of a few basic titles, but rather by pointing out to the student the necessity for the preliminary process of analysis which will enable him to define his bibliographic needs in intelligible terms. Such a procedure, even though it may mean sending the inquirer back to his thesis director, will eliminate much sloppy and ineffectual work at the graduate level. To the mature scholar, or student who has learned to define adequately his bibliographic needs, the librarian can give assistance in

(1) locating promising <u>collections</u> of source materials through such guides as

    (a) Library directories: <u>The American Library Directory</u>, 1948. compiled by Karl Brown. New York: Bowker Co., 1948; Special Libraries Association, <u>Special Library Resources</u>. 4 vol. Compiled by Rose Vormelker. New York: Special Libraries Association, 1941-47.

    (b) Surveys of library resources: Robert B. Downs. <u>Resources of Southern Libraries, A Survey of Facilities for Research.</u> Chicago: American Library Association, 1938. Philadelphia Bibliographical Planning Committee. <u>A Faculty Survey of the University of Pennsylvania Libraries.</u> Philadelphia: University of Pennsylvania Press, 1940; Karl Brown, ed. <u>A Guide to the Reference Collections of the New York Public Library.</u> New York: The New York Public Library, 1941. Robert B. Downs, <u>Resources of New York City Libraries, a Survey of Facilities for Advanced Study and Research.</u> Chicago: American Library Association, 1942.

(2) locating copies of <u>titles</u> known to be useful, but unavailable locally, through such instruments as:

    (a) National Union Catalog, Library of Congress, Washington, D. C.

    (b) Regional bibliographic centers, such as those at Philadelphia, Denver, Pacific Northwest.

    (c) Bibliographies which indicate locations: <u>Union List of Serials</u>; Charles Evans, <u>American Bibliography.</u> ... Chicago: Privately printed for the author by Blakely, 1903-34. 12 v.; Joseph Sabin, <u>Bibliotheca Americana.</u> ... New York: Sabin, 1868-92. Bibliographical Society of America, 1928-36. Vol. 1-24.

(3) obtaining through inter-library loan, photostat, microfilm, or other photographic processes, those volumes that are so available; and

(4) verifying bibliographic citations and details in bibliographic tools such as major library catalogs, bibliographies, etc., and by finding descriptions of best editions.

When the investigation reaches the evidence-gathering stage the librarian is likely to be called upon for specific factual information. The types of questions and the tools most appropriate for the answering of such questions may be broadly classified as in the following columns:

Agents:

Individuals	Directories, biographical dictionaries, genealogies, biographies, journals, correspondence, etc.
Organizations: Governmental, industrial, financial, professional, religious, etc.	Directories, histories of the particular organization or of the field to which it belongs, general histories of the place and period, official records both public and private, etc.

Events:

Dates, places, participants, accurate recital of the course of action, relation to other happenings, consequences.	Chronologies, general histories, particular histories, newspapers, diaries, biographies, official records, compilations of treaties, legal decisions, etc.

Interpretation:

Opinion as to causes, influences, underlying forces, larger consequences, psychological or philosophical explanations, etc.	General histories representing different points of view, biographies of participants, philosophies of history, etc.

Quantitative Description of:

Population, production, trade, social conditions, etc.	Statistical compilations and handbooks, special statistical analyses (monographs, journal articles, theses, etc.)

A brief but excellent analysis of the planning of a particular project is given by Charles A. Beard in the second chapter of his An Economic Interpretation of the Constitution of the United States.[6]

6

Charles A. Beard. An Economic Interpretation of the Constitution of the United States. (N. Y.: Macmillan, 1941). 330 pp.

What has been said, in the preceding paragraphs, about the general methods of procedure, modes of operation, and use of libraries by the historian may best be understood by referring to an actual situation. To this end Foundations of the Public Library (Chicago: University of Chicago Press, 1949) has been selected for analysis as a case study. The choice of this particular title has not been made because it exemplifies any unusual degree of excellence in its execution, or even because it is typical of the historian's modus operandi. Rather, this bit of egocentrism may be excused on the grounds that the study does deal with library history from a point of view which, at the time of its initiation, was something of an innovation, and also it is, of course, the one attempt at historical scholarship about which the present author can speak with first-hand knowledge.

Case Study of Investigation in Library History

Until 1938 the writing of library history, in the United States and elsewhere, had followed certain definite and stereotyped patterns: the history of libraries had largely been written as the biographies of individual institutions or of individual librarians. That such biographies were occasionally welded into a unified narrative concerning a place, region, country, or period of time did not alter the basic pattern. In 1931 Arnold K. Borden published in the first volume of the Library Quarterly a brief essay entitled "The Sociological Beginnings of the Library Movement"[7] in which he argued for a type of library history that would present the public library as a social agency conditioned by its social milieu. Four years later, in 1935, Carleton B. Joeckel clearly demonstrated the values of such an approach in the opening chapter of his Government of the American Public Library.[8] But the writing of library history continued to be mainly anecdotal and completely unsynthesized.

The decision of the present writer to follow the course proposed by Borden and Joeckel was influenced by a number of factors: (1) a period of graduate study in English and American literature which revealed the importance of interpreting literature in sociological as well as aesthetic terms, a point of view that was crystallized by the appearance of Vernon L. Parrington's Main Currents of American Thought; (2) a decade of professional experience as bibliographer and research assistant in a special library serving the staff of a research foundation for the investigation of population problems, a position which enabled him to become reasonably familiar with the techniques of research in both sociology and history; (3) the impact of the great depression of

---

[7]
Arnold K. Borden. "The Sociological Beginnings of the Library Movement," Library Quarterly, 1: 278-82, July 1931.

[8]
Carleton B. Joeckel. Government of the American Public Library. (Chicago: University of Chicago Press, 1935). 393 pp.

the 1930's upon libraries, which furnished ample evidence that the library did not exist in vacuo but was completely dependent upon the economic and social structure of which it was a part; and (4) the influence of the writings of Borden and Joeckel.

An exhaustive literature search was hardly essential since the author was already sufficiently familiar with such writings to be confident of the soundness of his position. Nevertheless, a complete re-examination of the literature of library history in general, and American library history in particular, confirmed his belief that the field was entirely unexploited. This search, however, eventually led to the publication of a bibliographic essay entitled "The Literature of American Library History," which not only analyzed the major contributions to the subject, but also attempted to relate the writing of American library history to the writings of American history in general during the same period. [9]

The major hypothesis was almost self-revealing. Simply stated, it was that, through an analysis of the historical evidence, it is possible to show that the emergence and development of the American public library was conditioned, either directly or indirectly, by the totality of forces that constitute the contemporary social milieu, and hence the public library is revealed as one of a number of social agencies brought into being by and shaped according to a constellation of specific social needs. The choice of region was equally evident, for the work of the antiquarians had already demonstrated that New England was, in almost every sense, the cradle of American librarianship. Obviously, also, a time span had to be defined in order to keep the investigation within manageable limits. Therefore, the decision was more or less arbitrarily made to terminate the study with the founding of the Boston Public Library in the middle of the nineteenth century, as Boston was the first American metropolis to establish a truly public library that was sponsored, encouraged, and ultimately largely supported by the municipal government.

The problem of sources raised vast and perplexing questions for one would need to ferret out materials which had not been used in this way before and hence the true nature of their contents was unknown. Furthermore, the very existence of certain types of documents was not an established fact. The types of materials needed, with appended examples, may best be presented in tabular form, and the secondary sources will be listed first since, in general, they were so consulted. Only a few examples of each type can be listed here; the complete list would contain hundreds of titles.

Secondary Sources:

General Histories of Colonial America and the United States:

9

Jesse H. Shera. "The Literature of American Library History" Library Quarterly, v. 15, no. 1 (January 1945) pp. 1-24.

Andrews, Charles M. The Colonial Period of American History. New Haven: Yale Univ. Press, 1934-   4 v.
Morison, Samuel Eliot and Commager, Henry Steele. Growth of the American Republic. New York: Oxford Univ. Press, 1930-   later editions.
Beard, Charles A. and Mary. Rise of American Civilization. N. Y.: Macmillan. 2 v.

General Histories of New England:

Adams, James Truslow. The History of New England. Boston: Little, Brown, 1927-   3 v.

Histories of Special Aspects of American Life, Either for the Country Generally or for New England Particularly:

Fish, Carl R. The Rise of the Common Man. N. Y.: Macmillan, 1927. (History of American Life Series. v. VI)
Cubberley, Ellwood P. Public Education in the United States. Boston: Houghton Mifflin, 1934.
Clark, Victor S. A History of Manufactures in the United States. N. Y.: McGraw-Hill, 1929. 3 v.
Wilson, Harold Fisher. The Hill Country of Northern New England. N. Y.: Columbia Univ. Press, 1936.
Wright, Thomas G. Literary Culture of Early New England. New Haven: Yale Univ. Press, 1920.
Morison, Samuel Eliot. The Maritime History of Massachusetts. Boston: Houghton Mifflin, 1941.
_____. The Puritan Pronaos. N. Y.: New York Univ. Press, 1936.
Ford, Washington C. The Boston Book Market, 1679-1700. Boston: The Club of Odd Volumes, 1917.

Histories of Individual Libraries:

Mason, George C. Annals of the Redwood Library. Newport, R. I.: The Redwood Library, 1891.
Wadlin, Horace G. The Public Library of the City of Boston, A History. Boston: The Trustees of the Boston Public Library, 1911.

Biographies of Librarians:

Shaw, Robert K. Samuel Swett Green. Chicago: American Library Association, 1926. (American Library Pioneers Series. v. II)

Government Publications (Secondary Sources):

Jewett, Charles C. Notices of Public Libraries ... Washington, D. C. Printed for the House of Representatives, 1851.

Massachusetts. Public Library Commission. Ninth Report.
Free Public Libraries in Massachusetts, 1899. Boston:
Wright & Potter, 1899. (Public Document no. 44)

U. S. Bureau of Education. Public Libraries in the United
States ... Washington, D. C.: Government Printing Office,
1876.

County and Local Histories of the New England Region:

These were searched for all references to libraries established
before 1855.

Exclusive of the county and local histories, which will be considered separately, approximately 350 titles were used as secondary
sources, which means, of course, that considerably more were inspected for possible utility but were rejected. Knowledge of these materials was obtained in seven different ways:

1. General bibliographies and periodical indexes.

2. Library catalogues.

3. Special bibliographies, such as the admirable "Critical Essay
   on Authorities" appended to each volume of the History of
   American Life Series.

4. Footnote citations in works consulted. This is a cumulative
   process and, together with the three previous sources, probably
   accounts for at least 60% of all materials used.

5. Communication with others having knowledge of the field, or
   of its component parts, either through conversation, formal
   interview, or correspondence. This probably accounts for 25%
   of all materials used, but its value is greater than this proportion would indicate as such expertly selective recommendations
   are likely to be the cream of the relevant literature.

6. Trade bibliographies, publishers' announcements, current
   book reviews -- of value only for the discovery of the most recent scholarship.

7. Browsing in the appropriate sections of library stacks, a procedure which, for this writer, has always proved astonishingly
   fruitful.

Finally, it should be pointed out that the use of secondary sources does
not terminate at any point during the course of the investigation, but
is a continuing process, which goes on even while the final copy is being prepared for the printer. The utility of the basic data is eventually exhausted, but the secondary sources are an almost inexhaustible
source of information.

Primary Sources:

These, like the secondary sources, may be described in certain well-defined categories.

Records of the Individual Libraries:

This most important single primary source is a great mass of published and unpublished materials relating to the libraries established in New England during the period covered by the study. It is composed of: acts of incorporation, annual reports, minutes of board meetings, catalogues, circulation records, acquisition lists, membership rosters, announcements, etc. Most of it was available only by visiting the libraries themselves or the repositories of such materials in the major research institutions. Much of it is uncatalogued and becomes available only through searching under the direction of, or at least with the advice of the librarian or curator in charge. This most important corpus of materials is least adequately charted bibliographically.

Government Documents (Primary Sources):

a. Federal -- Censuses, 1790-1860.
b. State -- Acts and Proceedings of the Legislatures of the six New England States.
c. Municipal -- ordinances, etc.

Contemporary Newspapers:

Many, especially those for Boston, contained editorial and other comment on library promotion and establishment.

Autobiographical Materials of Early Librarians:

This would have been a very valuable source did it exist in any quantity, but unfortunately the librarians of this period left behind very little personal record. There were, of course, very few librarians in the modern sense before 1855.

Autobiographical Materials of Men in Public Life Who Were Actively interested in Library Promotion:

An important source that includes the writings of such men as Benjamin Franklin, Henry Barnard, Horace Mann, George Ticknor, Edward Everett, etc.

Miscellaneous Fugitive Materials:

This includes such documents as handbills, announcements, advertisements, circulars, etc. Here, again, the course is bibliographically uncharted and much of it is acquired fortuitously, buried in dust-covered boxes or files, framed and hung on the wall, or, even, as in the case of the manuscript records of the Book Company of Durham, Connecticut, in the possession of a private family, the descendents of one of the founders.

Having defined the problem, established the hypotheses, and identified the major sources, both primary and secondary, the next step was the accumulation of the basic data relating to all available facts concerning every discoverable library established in New England during the time-span covered by the investigation. This was to be later assembled in a definitive card file, chronologically arranged, and showing in outline form all authenticated facts with appropriate citations of authorities. This file eventually included data on over one thousand such institutions. The work was initiated by a thorough search through all available local histories of New England for any reference to libraries established in their respective communities before 1855. This search was begun at the University of Chicago Library, continued at the Newberry Library which has an unusually fine local history collection, and ultimately extended to the library centers of the East, particularly the libraries of the state historical societies of New England.

Access to this material was most expeditiously gained through the shelf-lists of the libraries consulted, inasmuch as local history is a discrete category in modern library classifications, and the entire library holdings in this area are thus brought together in one place. In the Dewey scheme this would be numbers 974.1 through 974.6, in the Library of Congress classification, classes F1 through F105. Actually the search began with the books themselves as they stood on the shelves, and the titles thus obtained were later checked against the shelf-list in order to discover any titles that might have been in circulation when the original search was made. Eventually the bibliography of histories inspected was checked against Thomas L. Bradford's Bibliographer's Manual of American History[10] ... for further omissions. Approximately five hundred such histories were inspected.

The data extracted from these histories, together with similar information from such compilations as Charles C. Jewett's Notices of Public Libraries ... [11], and William J. Rhees' Manual of Public Li-

---

10
    Thomas L. Bradford. Bibliographer's Manual of American History. (Philadelphia: Hénkels, 1907-1910.) 3 v.
    11
    Charles C. Jewett. Notices of Public Libraries ... (Washington, D. C. Printed for the House of Representatives, 1851). 207 pp.

braries ... [12], and that segment of library literature that can be formally denominated library history, not only supplied a large portion of the necessary information needed for the structure of the study but also made it possible to determine just where in New England early library records might logically be expected to have been preserved. Thus an itinerary for a three months' period of study in New England was prepared. It included not only those towns where original records were most likely to be found, but also such major research collections in American history as those of the American Antiquarian Society, the John Carter Brown Library, the Boston Public Library, the Boston Athenaeum, the Library of Harvard University, the state libraries and the libraries of the state historical societies of the six New England states. This itinerary was further refined by correspondence with the librarians of those places the author planned to visit.

At this point the course of action became much less clear and the chase, therefore, the more exciting. The writer well remembers those hours of uncertainty on the train from Chicago to Worcester and the nagging fear that it all might prove to be a profitless venture. The boundaries of the familiar terrain had been crossed and in the distance there stretched only strange and unfamiliar land. No longer were there any bibliographic guides or landmarks to direct the intrepid explorer. He had no resources other than his inventiveness, perspicacity, and imagination, aided, perhaps by an occasional bit of good luck. Library catalogues often did not exist for the collections he would be examining, and when they did they failed to include the materials he needed or to analyze them in any way useful to him. The librarian and his personal knowledge of his collections was the only real point of entry to the storehouse of potentially useful record, and if he insisted that there was nothing, then one had no alternative but to accept the verdict. One librarian in particular was especially adamant, she had nothing "that would be of the slightest interest or use," but after an extended discussion on regional differences in porcine dietary habits, a subject in which she displayed considerable interest and competence, she brought forth a manuscript letter that was a real "find." For such a gem, the writer would gladly have talked for another hour about the virtues of "slop," "swill," or protein supplement!

Viewed in retrospect, after the passage of a decade: How can one generalize about librarians and their behavior when confronted by a problem in historical research in the very field with which they are supposed to be most familiar? Almost without exception they were pleasant, interested, and eager to be helpful; but enthusiasm is not enough. No more than two or three, and they were themselves scholars of established reputations, really understood the problems that confronted the investigator, or were able to translate those problems into acceptable bibliographic or documentary terms. Often they did not know the

---

12
    William J. Rhees, Manual of Public Libraries ... (Philadelphia: J. P. Lippincott, 1859). 687 pp.

resources of their own collections even when those collections were relatively small. On more than one occasion the writer was able, after only superficial examination, to point out the value of materials of which the librarian had been completely unaware. Almost always there was an excessive preoccupation with the anecdotal and with the antiquarian. This is not an implicit criticism of these librarians, it is a condemnation of an inadequate philosophy of librarianship and the ends it seeks to serve. These people had not been trained as scholars and they had not been taught to regard librarianship as a process of bibliographic organization. In short, the very reason why librarianship itself had come into existence had been lost from sight in a period of library education that imparted only techniques.

The data collected, the tasks that remained were those of assembly and organization, of analysis, and of interpretation. Finally, there was, of course, the actual writing of the manuscript. As this is not intended to be a text on the methods of historical research or a manual on how to write a research monograph, these portions of the process will only be mentioned in passing. One should point out, however, that the original plan of organization of the study was abandoned. At the beginning it was anticipated that the final text would be organized in a series of chapters each dealing with a major influence that contributed to the promotion of libraries, e. g., economic ability, education, philanthropy, historical scholarship, religion, etc. But the data so shaped itself that this outline emerged as only the outline of the concluding summary chapter. An approach through chronology and type of library organization eventually seemed to provide a more acceptable pattern. Hence maps, charts, and diagrams were prepared to show the configuration of library development throughout the period included in the study. The chapter on the circulating library was not even foreseen when the work was originally planned. Thus does the data itself largely determine the course of the investigation and the form of the result. As the exploration proceeds new avenues of approach appear and old paths are abandoned, certain elements are excluded because supporting evidence is not available and new facets are explored because of unexpected discoveries. When asked why he did not include Christobel along with Kubla Khan and the Ancient Mariner in The Road to Xanadu, John Livingstone Lowes replied simply, "because Christobel did not include itself." Because of the nature of the evidence, no one can foresee at the outset the exact course an historical investigation will take. The real test of scholarship is to manipulate the available materials in the best way possible to produce the most nearly accurate results.

Perhaps such a case study, even when it is reconstructed after the lapse of more than a decade, can tell one something about the operations of historical scholarship and the bibliographic requirements that they evoke. But much more would be gained if memory were not the only source of knowledge. What is needed is a series of case studies, documented from carefully recorded diaries from which could be evolved a body of authentic information concerning the methods of scholarship, the demands they place or could place upon library resource and the most effective techniques of bibliothecal organization that might be devised to meet those demands. Only through such careful investigation and analysis can the place of the library be adequately assessed in relation to the transmission of information within the world of scholarship. This is an almost unexplored area of library research, virgin soil for younger library investigators to cultivate.

CHAPTER VI

THE EDUCATOR AND HISTORY

In the introduction to this work it was pointed out that there are
no technologists or administrators operating in the field of history
as there are in the other branches of the social sciences, and therefore the librarian need be concerned with the provision of library and
bibliographic facilities only "for those scholars engaged in the writing
of history, for educators and students at all levels, and for members
of the general public."[1] There is no sharp division among even these
three groups, and any line of demarcation that does exist has been
less sharp in the past than it is today. Up to this point we have been
concerned chiefly with the work of the scholar in history.

The work of the educator in the field of history inevitably depends
upon and is derived from the work of the scholar, the relationship
being closest at the highest educational level and most remote at the
lowest level at which history is taught. However, in addition to the
substantive material and the points of view drawn from history, the
educator needs whatever information is currently available regarding
methods of teaching history and reliable materials to be used with
students at the level with which he is concerned. This information is
the proper province of the Education Library and may be located through
those bibliographic tools designed primarily to give access to the formal
literature of education.

At the highest level, that of professional specialization, the library
needs of the student are basically the same as those of the mature historian, this is especially true since the introduction of the seminar
method of teaching. In fact, more than a few graduate students of history have published the results of their seminar researches as important contributions to their special fields of interest. History can
not be effectively taught at this level without access to large collections of both secondary and primary source material, although microfilm and microcard reproduction are rapidly becoming important allies
in extending the resources of hitherto inadequate collections. As dependence upon local resources alone decreases, the necessity and the
usefulness of bibliographic guides increase, and the librarian will
do well to be as generous as possible in the provision of such aids.
Inter-library specialization and co-operation are the only answers to
the growing demands of scholarship. The personal assistance which
may be requested of the librarian by the graduate student will also

---

1

approximate the demands of the mature historian, so that all of the points raised in the discussion of the work of the scholar will also be applicable to those exploring, for the first time, the vast uncharted seas of original research.

The problems of library acquisition policy raised by the needs of the scholar and advanced research student are very acute, and their solution can be reduced to no simple formula. The omnivorous collecting of _all_ possible materials is now almost universally acknowledged to be an impracticable and an undesirable procedure. The creation at the University of Chicago of the Midwest Inter-Library Center wherein are deposited the little-used, but non-the-less valuable resources of research drawn from the collections of some fifteen major university libraries, is an overt recognition of the need for cooperation among such libraries in the building of their acquisition programs. These concentrated masses of materials again emphasize the importance for more adequate bibliographic organization to make their resources available, and indeed this need has been recognized in the increasing attention given to its bibliographic equipment and services by M. I. L. C. Similarly the inauguration of the Farmington Plan, whereby a group of major research libraries have voluntarily agreed to limit their acquisition programs to certain specified subject fields, signifies the decline of the old doctrine of institutional isolation in the development of research collections.

As these cooperative undertakings grow -- as indeed they must if society is to avoid bibliothecal innundation -- traditional library practices and procedures, especially in cataloging and classification, must give way to new and greatly modified techniques for bibliographic organization. The problem for the "depository" library becomes somewhat more archival than bibliothecal, and graphic records must be described or calendared as "blocks" or "segments" of collections, rather than in terms of minute description of individual titles. Similarly national and regional union listings will then become the supporting structure of the bibliographic system.

So far as the individual library is concerned, little can be done beyond the identification for each institution of three areas of acquisitions policy:

1. Those materials directly related to the immediate instructional program of the school. These are relatively few in number and, to the extent that obsolete materials can be replaced with more recent publications, the total number of titles can be made to remain relatively constant.
2. Those research areas in which the collections of the academic library must be adequate to the demands of the faculty and graduate students, but need not be outstandingly extensive.
3. Those few areas in which the collection should be definitely superior. Too frequently the choices here are fortuitous, arising from a gift or series of gifts, the demands of a particularly vocal faculty member, or some other purely local determinant. Fortunate indeed is the librarian who has the freedom and the resources

104

to permit him to chart his own course, and to determine rationally for himself these areas of concentration.

In all of these areas the growth of the collections in most academic libraries is generally conditioned by: (a) the personal enthusiasms of individual instructors; (b) the state and condition of the second-hand book market at any given moment; and (c) the freedom of the librarian and his aids to control the expenditure of the funds available. Beyond these, one may isolate certain types of materials for more explicit comment.

Manuscripts: Though in many areas of historical investigation manuscripts are a basic source, few libraries can afford the luxury of extensive manuscript collections. Though their values are great their costs of acquisition, organization, and servicing are high. Some modest collecting is, however, imperative for any institution offering graduate courses in historical research, if for no other purpose than to offer the student an opportunity to become familiar at first hand with the problems encountered by the investigator in dealing with this kind of material. Further, the preservation of manuscript materials of importance locally is probably a social responsibility of the institution. The value of the microfilm in extending the utility of the manuscript is, of course, obvious; but in most situations involving research at the level of the doctorate and above, the interests of scholarship are probably best served by making travel funds available so that the investigator can personally inspect those places where the concentration of his sources is greatest.

Newspapers: The importance of the newspaper to the historian has been dealt with elsewhere. [2] However, enthusiasm for the microfilm must not obscure the fact that, while it offers important aid in solving problems of storage and preservation, it contributes relatively little to the solution of acquisition problems. In the past, academic libraries have probably tended to collect with too great abandon extensive files of newspapers, and in many libraries these long files, even on microfilm, have become a real drain upon the resources of their owners. Cooperative depositories offer only limited relief, and the present uncoordinated pattern of newspaper preservation cannot long be continued without serious consequences to all concerned. Though the major use of newspapers seems to be concentrated in the research and reference libraries, attempts on the part of such agencies to preserve extensive files of these materials are imposing a serious financial burden that may soon become excessive. The rapid deterioration of wood-pulp will automatically solve the problem if no rational solution is devised.

Decentralization of newspaper holdings, with the area of origin as

---
2

the focus, would seem to be indicated. The research institutions which are finding the maintenance of newspaper files an oppressive responsibility should be encouraged to distribute their holdings to the appropriate local areas, and the public libraries of many communities, working with the cooperation and financial assistance of the publishers, might well become the depositories for preserving the newspapers of their localities. Inasmuch as the needs of the scholar for this type of material are so ill defined and so imperfectly understood, no real progress in solving the problems of newspaper acquisition can be made until more adequate research has been carried out, preferably by the library schools. Such a research program might attack the problem (1) by an analysis of the writings in American local history to determine the extent and character of newspaper use by historians; (2) by an analysis of library use of newspapers directed toward the discovery of the uses to which newspapers are put by library patrons; and (3) by the investigation of problems of the bibliographic organization of the press to discover the degree to which inadequate indexing discourages newspaper use. [3]

Rare Books: Misapprehension concerning the utility of "rare books" to the historical scholar is so wide-spread that some consideration of this class of materials is desirable. No one has yet adequately defined "rare books." In the generic sense a "rare book" is, by definition, any book that is "rare," scarce, or for any reason difficult to replace, and hence requires special handling to preserve it from destruction, loss, or unnecessary wear. In this sense, then, "rare books" are probably more extensively used by historians than by most other scholars. But in librarianship and in the book-trade "rare book" is more frequently understood as synonymous with "collector's item," first edition, limited edition, or "association copy," and the value of these to the historian has been greatly exaggerated. Admittedly, there are times when the scholar will find it useful, even imperative, to examine the treasures of the bibliophile, but contrary to the views of many, the accumulation of these "museum pieces" does not promote research on the part of the library clientele. One may derive a certain esthetic or sensuous pleasure from viewing or handling the Gutenberg Bible, The Bay Psalm Book, or The New England Primer, but how does one make use of it in "research," and what values does it engender other than pride of ownership?

About 1937 the American Historical Association, through the generosity of the Detroit bibliophile, Tracy W. McGregor, made available to liberal arts colleges throughout the country funds to be used for the purchase of rare Americana. [4] These donations were awarded in the

---

3

See Jesse H. Shera. "The Preservation of Local Illinois Newspapers." I. L. A. Record. v. 5, no. 3, (March 1952) pp. 49-52.

4

American Historical Association. Committee on Americana for College Libraries, The McGregor Plan. (Ann Arbor: The Committee, 1937). 15 pp.

hope that the rare books thus acquired would encourage investigation into the American past. That the McGregor Fund exerted little influence upon American historical scholarship is hardly surprising. Had these funds been used for the acquisition of local or regional source materials which otherwise were threatened by neglect or loss, or had they been given as grants-in-aid for research in American history, the benefits to historical scholarship would have been markedly greater. But the purchase, by the average college library, of a first edition of Bradford's Plymouth Plantation, especially when inexpensive and thoroughly adequate reprints are easily available, is a form of bibliographic conspicuous consumption that most librarians would do well to avoid.

Below this most advanced level, the teacher of history will have only as much latitude in the choice of materials, methods, and even points of view, as the parent institution permits. States, municipalities, and even independent private institutions usually establish curricula to which the individual teacher must conform, although such curricula vary widely in the extent of control exercised over them. Every good educational library maintains files of sample curricula, course outlines, and lists of recommended books and materials. In general, there has been a movement away from adherence to a single text in the teaching of history and increasing reliance upon scattered readings, although the text remains the backbone of most courses. The compilation of source readings into single volumes may mean no more than the development of a new kind of text, with no greater freedom on the part of the teacher to choose his own materials.[5] However great or small this freedom of choice may be, there will always be some need for a continuing stream of bibliographies of suitable materials, which the librarian may provide from among those listed in the Education Index or in the Bibliographic Index. Such bibliographies will supplement the basic selection aids, such as the Standard Catalog for High School (or Elementary School) Libraries, Shaw's List of Books for College Libraries, etc., in the choice of formal histories, biographies of historical characters, and historical fiction to be added to the library collection. Whether or not he is a member of the curriculum-planning committee (as he should be) the librarian must constantly consult with the teaching staff in order to keep in touch with current trends in methods and materials, and to contribute his own specialized knowledge toward the formulation of a program which will ensure the most effective use of all available materials, audio-visual as well as graphic.

The extent to which modern courses in social studies have depended upon history as a framework within which to fit the study of contemporary social problems is evident in two recent yearbooks of the National Council for Social Studies, the Seventeenth Yearbook, 1947, devoted to

---

5

For an example of such a compilation, see:
Chicago University College Staff. Social Science I. The People Shall Judge. (Chicago: Univ. of Chicago Press, 1950) 2 v.

the teaching of American history, and the Twentieth Yearbook, 1949, on the teaching of world history. [6] The latter volume contains three chapters particularly relevant to our purpose, with good lists of bibliographic aids:

Babcock, Chester D. "Reading Materials for the Secondary Schools," pp. 153-172.
Brooks, Alice R. "Reading Materials for the Elementary School," pp. 173-185.
Tyrrell, William G. "Audio-Visual Materials for World History," pp. 186-210.

This dependence of the social studies upon the framework of history should intensify the child's awareness of the importance of historical knowledge to an understanding of man's relation to his fellow men, and should further the integration of history with the other sciences of society.

---

[6]
Washington, D. C.: The National Council for Social Studies, 1947 and 1949

CHAPTER VII

THE GENERAL READER AND HISTORY

In the preceding pages we have examined the activities of the scholar in developing historical insights and the function of the educator in transmitting these insights to the younger generation. The work of these two groups may be considered successful only to the extent that they stimulate a mature ability to use historical materials and historical interpretations in the making of the many decisions required of every citizen in the course of his mature participation in the life of his community, and in the exercise of his duties as a responsible citizen.

In this chain of transmission from scholar to general reader the librarian has the opportunity to play a really creative role. The purposes of the general reader are always individual rather than social, but the librarian, while making every effort to meet these individual needs and desires, attempts to broaden them in such a way that they will contribute to the wise solution of current social problems and to the integration of the individual into the life of the group. History for its own sake may be the point of departure for the general reader, but if the pursuit of a knowledge of history remains a mere enthusiasm for the dramatic, the sensational, and the anecdotal, the strivings of the scholar toward valid insights into the past are a vain and futile endeavor.

The popularity of history with the adult reading public is a well established phenomenon. More than any other academic discipline it has aroused the active interest of the layman, and even among younger readers it is surpassed only by the current widespread enthusiasm for science. The reasons for this general absorption in the past are not difficult to distinguish. Basically it satisfies a universal need for vicarious adventure, and, inasmuch as man's struggles with nature and against other men have for centuries been the very stuff of historical writing, such narratives have offered an obvious escape from the tedium of daily life. Similarly, history offers an escape from reality into a romantic world in which the troubles of the present may be forgotten -- a world that promises hope for the future -- a world in which, though heroes are beset with vicissitudes and seemingly insurmountable difficulties, virtue ultimately triumphs, evil is crushed, and everything always eventually "works out all right."

From history, too, man achieves a sense of identity with the past, an enlargement and enrichment of his own personality through the discovery of his own place in the historical continuum. In its pages he finds both similarities and sharp contrasts, and comes to realize that there were others who have been confronted by and have surmounted difficulties not unlike his own, or that there were those whose lot was

109

far more desperate than his. In history there is both a diminution of his own misfortunes and an elevation of his prowess. He sees in the weaknesses of Caesar his own weaknesses, and not only shares in the conquests of Tamburlaine, but for a time himself becomes Tamburlaine and rides "in triumph through Persepolis." But such identification can be more than a romantic attachment to the heroes of another day. In its less spectacular manifestations it becomes a real enrichment of the individual's environment through conscious inclusion of what he has actually inherited from the past. The past, thus, in a very real sense becomes part of the entirety of his social milieu.

From history comes a better understanding of the present as the result of past forces, a true sense of historicity that may eventually take shape in the search for universal laws or philosophical principles that may have prognostic values. The scholar may deny that Clio has the right to assume the prerogatives of Cassandra, but nevertheless the general reader instinctively turns to history as a reliable guide to present policy and action, a faith that is not always justified and may be potentially dangerous and misleading, but which for many still remains the only real justification for the historian's toil. Similarly, one may turn to history for a rationale for a desired course of action in the present, and though caution may warn that historical analogy is beset with pitfalls, the argument is convincing.

To say that curiosity is one of man's strongest attributes, is indeed platitudinous, but an antiquarian curiosity about distant places and times is one of the strongest urges that impels the general reader to the literature of history. Basically, this is doubtless another manifestation of the ubiquitous need for the enrichment of experience, and to a certain extent, at least, it represents a retreat from the present into vicarious adventure. But shorn of its more subtle motives, it remains a desire for knowledge for its own sake, an avocation that prompts the not-too-tired businessman to investigate for himself the way in which the Ghost Dance War got its name, or whether Custer actually disobeyed Terry's orders, and to what extent he really was responsible for the defeat of the Seventh Cavalry at the Battle of the Little Big Horn. This preoccupation with the antiquarian is essentially the attraction of narrative, the appeal of anecdote, the love of a good story. All these represent very human traits which the skillful librarian can convert into a real appreciation for the more important values that history has to offer the layman.

Much of the public interest in history is a result of the conditioning processes of early schooling. The emphasis, either direct or indirect, that history has received from teachers and librarians in the grammar and secondary schools has promoted a taste for history and a real, though often vaguely understood, awareness of its importance; and this, for many people, continues into later life. Thus the average individual emerges from his formal training with the belief that history is a vital element in the intellectual equipment of every educated person. From this preconditioning arises the popular assumption that knowledge of history has prestige value. For if an understanding of history contributes to the wisdom of the educated man then it must logically follow that the educated man must be interested in history. The enthusiastic response that was accorded the translation of Spengler's Decline of the West in the decade of the 1920's, the rather surprising market that developed for the philosophical writings of Toynbee some twenty years later, and the economic feasibility of publishing Arthur Schlesinger's Age of Jackson in pocket-book format, all testify to the fact that probably more people evinced an interest in these works than were really capable of their comprehension. The writings of Spengler and Toynbee are certainly not easily comprehended by the lay mind, and Schlesinger's work presupposes a reasonably adequate understanding of early nineteenth century American history and politics, yet they all were widely discussed and extensively purchased, though it is difficult to believe that many readers had the stamina to pursue them through their final pages. The power of prestige as a motivating factor in promoting the reading of history is further exemplified by the popularity of capsule history and the vogue of such titles as Wells' Outline of History, which was a best seller in the 1920's.

The ability to comprehend broad historical generalization such as are contained in the works of Toynbee and Spengler represents a high level of sophistication in reading. The individual may begin his pursuit of history for one or more of the personal motives outlined above, but as he comes to identify himself with the innumerable personages about whom he reads, he gradually and almost imperceptibly becomes a part of a variety of social environments. If the author is skillful in the presentation of those details which emphasize the character of the period about which he writes, the reader senses the milieu and perceives the broader movements with a clarity which he does not get from the contemporary scene in which he is daily besieged by a mass of unselected details and pressures. From the vicarious experience derived through reading about a number of different historical situations he is able to take a more or less objective view of his own social environment, to see the outlines of its broader movements, and to sense their significance. The rationale for the public support of libraries by society is that society as a whole will benefit through the development of this kind of historical perspective on the part of a substantial number of its participating citizens. The librarian who is mindful of his social responsibility will, therefore, make every effort to select and interpret historical works which will promote this kind of social understanding.

From history the individual derives not only a more intelligent awareness of the society of which he is a part, but also a greater tolerance for societies that are unlike his own. As one may grow more patient with the idiosyncracies of one's neighbor through a knowledge of his past, so may a nation be more adequately prepared to understand the motives of an economic rival through an appreciation of the historic roots of that rivalry.

From historical consciousness derives also adaptability to change, an acute realization that life has not always been as it is today, and that it will not forever remain as it is at present. Thus one arrives at a proper perspective upon contemporary events, an ability to relate each to its appropriate antecedents and to project, at least to some extent, its possible consequences. History properly comprehended enriches and deepens the understanding of contemporary society.

But the fruits of history are not all nutritive. They can be, and indeed often are, poisonous in the extreme, and the results of historical investigation can very well be made to serve anti-social ends. For excessive preoccupation with history may breed an unwholesome veneration for the past, a defeatism, a predisposition to accept the present, a conviction that "the founding fathers knew best," and that only the reckless blunderer would change their handiwork. History is one of the most potent weapons of intense and uncompromising nationalism, and instead of promoting an understanding of the outlander it may engender hatred and even open conflict. "Of all the forms of pride," wrote Herder, "I hold national pride the most foolish; it ruined Greece, it ruined Judea and Rome!"

Even in its less fanatical manifestations historical analogy is treacherous. Historical situations are seldom as nearly identical as they superficially appear, and even the best-intentioned and most meticulous scholar may be led astray by the appearance of a historical parallel. Finally, there is danger in the fact that antiquarianism, pursued for its own sake, is itself an intellectual opiate, an easy retreat from reality, an intoxicant that inhibits effective and coordinated action in the present.

But history is amoral, it is inherently neither good nor bad. Only the abuses of history make it an instrument of reaction, retreat, or aggression. The task of the librarian, then, is to develop taste in historical writing that will insure against its degradation, and make of it an instrument for the advance of social welfare.

History and the Child

It is almost axiomatic that the foundations for taste in historical writing must be laid as early in the life of the individual as possible. The importance of history in the grammar school curriculum has already been indicated, but the school librarian can supplement the work of the classroom by directing students' attention to materials that are at once examples of accurate scholarship and at the same time appealing to the mind of the child. Publishers have flooded the market with capsule history written-down to the grammar school level, but the librarian would be well advised to view such titles with uncompromising skepticism. By contrast there are certain landmark titles with which every school librarian should be familiar and which can be used as standards against which other publications may be judged. The student is probably most easily introduced to meaningful history through historical fiction, in which, as in the case of Esther Forbes' Johnny Tremain, real historical characters, in this instance Paul Revere, are recreated, or through "period" stories, like Rachel Field's Hitty, Her First Hundred Years, or Elizabeth Gray's Adam of the Road, that give the reader a true feeling for a past period or epoch, but in which all the characters

are fictitious. Of the two forms the latter is probably the more successful inasmuch as it is difficult for even the most skillful literary crafts-
man to present historic personages in a convincing manner.

Progression in the reading of history might well continue through
the reading of biographies of historical figures, and indeed biography
is becoming increasingly important in the book stocks of the school librarian. American publishers have released a veritable flood of biographical materials, many of which are inferior in the extreme; probably no literary form at the juvenile level has been so exploited. Here
one might mention as among the best the works of Clara Judson on
Lincoln and Washington, which are appropriate for use in the middle and
upper elementary grades, and the distinguished work of Jeanette Eaton,
her life of Gandhi, and a proposed series on important Americans.
Miss Eaton's writings are appropriate for junior and senior high school
students. In formal history by far the most outstanding examples are
the works of Genevieve Foster, George Washington's World, Abraham
Lincoln's World, and Augustus Caesar's World, of which the last approaches the adult reading level, and Elizabeth C. Baity's Americans
Before Columbus. Finally, one should mention the importance of folk-
tales, which often give the reader a better insight into the characteristics of a culture than is possible from writing that is consciously historical. In this category Anne Malcolmson's Yankee Doodle's Cousins,
and the several collections compiled by Moritz Jagendorf are conspicuously successful. For further guidance the school as well as the
public librarian, should refer to

   Coan, Otis W. and Lillard, R. G. America in Fiction: an
Annotated List of Novels That Interpret Aspects of Life in the
United States. 3rd ed. Stanford University, California: Stanford
University Press, 1949. 196 pp.

   Logasa, Hannah. Historical Fiction and Other Reading References for Classes in Junior and Senior High Schools. 4th ed.
Philadelphia: McKinley Co., 1949. 193 pp.

The Children's Book Center of the University of Chicago publishes
a monthly list of children's books which have been carefully evaluated
and annotated according to grade level and appropriateness for various library purposes.

For adults who have acquired an interest in history relatively late
in life, and who have not been preconditioned to an appreciation of history through early formal education, the librarian will probably find the
same reading guidance pattern, progressing from historical fiction,
through biography, to formal history, effective. But the adult who will
persevere through this long and arduous path is relatively rare, for it
presupposes the awakening of an intense interest in history that is not
common among those who have failed to acquire enthusiasm for, or at
least an understanding of, the values of history during the formative
years. The librarian will probably be more successful if history is

associated with some outstanding contemporary event, a political controversy, a war, an economic depression, or even a currently popular movie or play that has a historic setting or historic overtones.

The ingenious librarian can make effective use of local historical groups to extend a central focus of antiquarian interest or curiosity and to arouse a more general and profitable concern with the past. Furthermore, the librarian would do well to concentrate library publicity upon materials that relate to a dramatic event or personality, rather than upon a specific title, for the library by its inability to stock more than a few copies of even the most popular individual titles can, on such a basis, never serve more than a relatively small portion of its entire potential clientele. But by relating an event to an entire body of relevant literature the scope of usefulness of the collection is immeasurably increased. Finally, one scarcely needs to point out that the librarian would be well advised to direct the interest of his patrons through the active promotion of titles that have vitality and literary merit, as well as historicity. Thus one is brought face to face with the criteria by which the writing of history for the general reader is to be judged.

Standards of Value

The problems of assessing the validity of scholarly historical writing has been considered at some length in the preceding sections, and the importance of the application of these criteria to historical writings appropriate to the needs of the general reader cannot be too strongly emphasized. The tests of truth are the same for all kinds of historical exposition. The real apposition, then, is not between history written for the general reader and history for the scholar, but between sound and unsound history for whatever audience the author may have had in mind. It is this distinction that the librarian must train himself to make. At this point, therefore, the discussion will be limited to certain general observations, not elsewhere considered, with somewhat more emphasis upon the writing of historical fiction and biography, since these two categories comprise a large proportion of the general public's reading of history.

There is, then, no sharp line of demarcation that separates historical writing for the scholar from that for the general reader. Admittedly, as has been pointed out above, there are types of historical exposition that do necessitate maturity of intellect for their adequate comprehension; but in history perhaps more than in any of the other social sciences, and certainly more than in the natural sciences, the general reader can assimilate writing of a high degree of conceptual difficulty. That this is so may be partly due to the fact that general history treats of phenomena and concepts that are more immediately familiar to the layman, and partly the result of the historian's relative success in avoiding the use of specialized jargon. This acceptance of history on the part of the general reader has been further promoted, during the past two or three decades, by the emergence of a substantial group of historical writers who are not professional historians in the sense of having had formal training in research methods in history. The substantial work of such lay scholars as Carl Sandburg, Claude Bowers, Robert E. Sherwood, Margaret Leech, and Esther Forbes, has had a wholesome influence upon historical scholarship, and has revived its literary significance. In their wake has come a renaissance of general interest in historical works that is reminiscent of the age of Bancroft, Parkman, and Prescott. For the "classical historians" of previous ages, be it remembered, were not writing for the benefit of some future academician who might use their work as the training ground for graduate students; they were writing for the general readers of their own time. They knew that the past survives and becomes a reality only when it is written about, and that a society which restricts historical knowledge to the monopoly of a few scholars will benefit but little from the records of the past.

Historical Fiction

But of all the literary forms for the encouragement of general interest in history, the novel is at once the most effective and potentially the most harmful. The virtues of a good historical novel in vitalizing the dry bones of historical fact, need hardly be labored here. Even the sophisticated reader gains better insights into the American past through the perusal of the pages of such literary treatments as Esther Forbes' Mirror for Witches and The Running of the Tide, Le Grand Cannon's Look to the Mountain, or the novels of Conrad Richter than is possible from most of the formal treatises on history. But historical fiction is not a substitute for historical exposition, and it is more than an easy introduction to formal historical writing. It has a substantial and important function of its own. Better than any other literary form, the historical novel can recreate the people, problems, passions, conflicts, motives, and social directions that impel the actions and decisions which more formal history has recorded. The great virtue of the good historical novel is that it gives psychological insights into the past actions of men and thus enables one better to understand the actions of men today.

The great danger of the historical novel, on the other hand, lies not only in the possible absence of true historicity, but in the possibility that it may become the vehicle for the destruction of those very historical attitudes that it should seek to engender. History in the historical novel may become quite incidental, but when it surrenders to the picaresque, the love of adventure for its own sake, the exploitation of sensationalism, the promotion of false social values, it is no longer a true historical novel, but only a tenth-rate story that happened to have its setting in a remote time or place.

Insofar, therefore, as the good historical novel is at once a contribution to historical knowledge and a literary achievement, the librarian in selecting such materials for his collections and in recommending them to his patrons is faced with the double task of applying the standards of historical scholarship and assessing literary merit. This probably means that the search for acceptable titles will be twice as arduous and the yield only half as great, but the rewards in satisfaction both to librarian and reader should justify the effort. [1]

Unfortunately, the bibliographic aids in this area are not particularly good. The bibliography of American historical fiction compiled by Coan and Lillard has already been mentioned. The index to the Book Review Digest is the most easily accessible and complete guide to novels about a particular place or period, and although it includes any title which has been considered worthy of review a selection may be made by references to the reviews themselves. Two older bibliographies of occasional usefulness are:

Baker, Ernest Albert. A Guide to Historical Fiction. N. Y.: Macmillan, 1914. 565 pp.

Nield, Jonathan. A Guide to the Best Historical Novels and Tales. 5th ed. N. Y.: Macmillan, 1929. 424 pp.

Though not a bibliography, the librarian will find helpful Leisy's study of the American historical novel, which lists and characterizes many works. [2]

Biography

Biography shares with fiction an important place in encouraging general interest in history, for like fiction, biography is dominantly narrative, episodic, and dramatic. In it, too, the psychological appeal is conspicuous and important, and, it, also, can clothe the skeleton of historical events with flesh and blood, and give to more formal history a human vitality. The recent importance of the political leader in the shaping of world events -- Roosevelt, Churchill, Hitler, Stalin -- has doubtless contributed to the popular revival of biography as a literary form. Similarly, the writing of formal biography by a group of able lay scholars has made available to the general reader a group of substantial works of unusually high literary and historical merit. Freeman's Robert E. Lee, Bowers' Beveridge and the Progressive Era,

---

[1] One should mention, at least in a foot-note, that historical fiction does not have to be written in prose. Stephen Vincent Benet's John Brown's Body and Western Star, the latter left unfinished at the time of his death, are outstanding examples of contemporary historical epics.

[2] Ernest E. Leisy. The American Historical Novel. (Norman: Univ. of Oklahoma Press, 1950). 280 pp.

Sandburg's Abraham Lincoln, and Pringle's Theodore Roosevelt, are conspicuous examples of excellence in biographical writing.

Standards of literary criticism and historical judgment are no different for biography than for other forms of historical writing. Here again the attention of the practicing librarian should be directed not only to the standard reviewing media, but to such special sources as the admirable and extensive review sections of such scholarly journals as The American Historical Review, The Mississippi Valley Historical Review, and The New England Quarterly.

As history is the bridge between the social sciences and the humanities, so biography and autobiography connect history with literature. Not only does biography clothe history in a living reality, but it is a vital necessity to history, including as it does all autobiography, reminiscences, memoirs, letters, and journals. Biography provides the very foundation stones of history itself and the early biographers were never quite certain whether they were writing biography or history or only a dissociated listing of events that to them seemed worthy of perpetuation. [3]

Nevertheless, the biographer, though he must work within the limits of actuality, must be inspired by the power of imagination, for basically biography is a literary form. It is perhaps not accidental that many of our most successful biographical works treat of literary figures, for it is natural that men of letters should write about other men of letters. Similarly, theologians tend to write about theologians, doctors about doctors, and men of science about scientists. Hence those fields of human activity which do not demand a high degree of literary competence tend to be neglected, and it has been only recently that leaders in commerce and industry have attracted the serious attention of biographers. Not until the present century did professional writers turn to biography as a profitable area for exploitation, and begin to search for colorful figures whose lives would make "good copy". At the other extreme, novelists have often cast their narratives in a form so close to biography that Henry Fielding, uncertain of a properly descriptive title for his greatest prose work, hit upon The History of Tom Jones. A further bond between biography and literature is the romans à clef, in which actual historical figures, including often even the author, appear in transparent disguise. Thus much biographical writing may be regarded as pure literature with slight historic value though some are important to the history of particular arts or sciences, while still other biographies may have value mainly as human documents from which one may derive new or revitalized psychological insights.

Of standards for judging the excellence of biographical exposition, much has been said either explicitly or implicitly, in the preceding pages. Here, perhaps, it is sufficient to point out that the essential property in biography is truth -- truth to the character of the human

---

3
Biographies of statesmen and other figures important to history itself have been discussed throughout the present work.

being portrayed, truth to the spirit of the age in which he lived. This means not only factual accuracy, but analysis and interpretation. A good biography must be not only true to the sequence of events, it must have a unity of presentation and of relevance to contemporary life, and it must display both poetic insight and critical detachment. In short, it is not a psychological case-study, but a work of art.

Many library inquirers, however, want not extended literary treatments but brief summaries of the facts of an individual's life. For this purpose the biographical dictionaries, such as Who's Who, Dictionary of American Biography, World Biography, Current Biography, etc., are most useful. The biographical dictionaries and professional directories of special fields are obvious sources. The general encyclopedias, especially the Encyclopedia of the Social Sciences, frequently give excellent scholarly evaluations of the work of an individual in science or letters, but the number of such biographical treatments is necessarily limited. Obituaries, which are indexed in the various periodical indexes, as well as in the Biography Index, are sometimes the only source of available information about the individual's contribution to his field, but they are of course not really evaluative. In this connection, it should be remembered that if the usual indexes fail to reveal any information, the journal of any association to which the individual belonged may have published an obituary. There is, of course, much biographical detail about various people buried in histories of a period or in the biographies of other individuals. The search for such details is arduous and the rewards are uncertain, but possibly no other type of reference question offers greater challenge to the ingenuity, the imagination and the stored book knowledge of the librarian.

Library patrons may pursue biography from one of two distinct approaches: (1) because they are concerned with the development of a particular subject field or special activity and desire information about the contribution of a certain individual to that development, or (2) because they find intellectual satisfaction in biography as a literary form. This dual approach to biography is reflected in two methods of classifying biography on the library shelves. The Dewey schedules class biography, individual, collective, and autobiography, in classes 920 to 928, in which 920.01 to 920.09 is assigned to general biography by nationality according to the mnemonic geographic breakdown, and 921 to 928 is reserved for biography of individuals arranged according to specific fields of activity. Thus the biography of a geologist would be classed in 925.5, as 550 is the Dewey number for geology. This method of classification has generally been rejected by librarians in favor of classifying biography directly in the subject concerned, e.g., the biography of a geologist would be assigned to class 550, that of an educator to 370, and the biographies of kings, presidents, and other figures prominently associated with the history of a place or nation would be classified in the appropriate category for the history of the country concerned. The use of this method, therefore, leaves 920 for only the biographies of individuals which cannot be assigned elsewhere, collective biographies of individuals active in a variety of different fields, and books on the art of biography as a literary form. Public and school libraries, however, often prefer to maintain a separate collection of biography where it can be inspected by those patrons who desire to read biography for its own sake, and here the practice is to class biography, either simply as 92, or as "B", arranged alphabetically by biographee and shelved where inspection by the library patron is encouraged. In such a system 920 would bring together only those works which treat of the art of writing biography. [4] Whatever the classification system employed, the customary practice in assigning book numbers is to cutter the title according to the biographee, followed by the initial, in lower case, of the last name of the author of the biography, e. g., Thayer's Life of Beethoven would be 780.92 - B415t or 920, 92, or B - B415t. In cataloging biography the name of the person written about appears as the subject heading, with the sub-division BIOGRAPHY AND CRITICISM if there is sufficient material in the library to justify subdivision. However, the term BIOGRAPHY is never used as an independent subject heading except for collective biography. Thus there is no place in the library catalogue where biography as a literary form is cumulated for the entire collection, nor will the shelf list serve as a substitute in libraries where biographies are classified with the subject field.

Although a great deal of historical scholarship must go into the writing of good biography, there is no separate scholarship of biographical writing itself. It draws its scholarship from the fields of literature and history and their related disciplines, psychology, political science, economics, anthropology, the fine arts, and the like. As an art form it reflects the changes in methods and points of view of the supporting disciplines, and it is particularly responsive to new approaches to history and to new trends in literary taste. These transitions in scholarship and taste are evident in the kinds of biography that have been produced during the last few centuries.

Classical biography emphasized the exploits, both actual and legendary, of great political and military leaders. The monastic chroniclers of the Christian world wrote of the early church fathers, whose human traits were effectively submerged in a flood of moralizing. The earliest English biographies were almost invariably the work of monks and schoolmen who wrote of the saints and their martyrdom. Even the work of the Venerable Bede was replete with ethical judgments and unquestioning acceptance of the miraculous. Bishop Asser's Life of Alfred the Great, which ranks as the first English biography of a layman, conveys little impression of the subject's real personality, but presents a didactic portrayal of the virtues of devoutness, industry, chastity, and learning.

With the sixteenth century came a revival of interest in biographical writing, though it expressed itself in the sensational martyrology of such

---

[4] See William S. Merrill. Code for Classifiers. 2nd ed. (Chicago: American Library Association, 1939) pp. 147-161.

collections as Foxe's Book of Martyrs, of which four editions were published in the author's lifetime. The seventeenth century brought some semblance of historical scholarship to biographical writing. Isaac Walton, in his Lives, was probably the first to make extensive use of letters written by his subjects and later William Mason's Life of Thomas Gray was the first to display a systematic use of such materials for the graphic portrayal of character. The term biography itself was first employed by Dryden in the preface to his translation of Plutarch, where he defined it as "the history of particular men's lives." With the acceptance of biography as a common literary form, it began to expand into a variety of types and points of view which have increased in number as new areas of scholarship and new fields of interest have opened new sources for exploitation. Fashions in biography may change, and new types may advance or decline in popularity, but biography as a generic literary form remains conspicuously popular.

The close affinity between biography and literature which has resulted in the production of so many important books about great literary figures may be illustrated by such titles as Boswell's Johnson and the journals and other papers of James Boswell, Johnson's Lives of the Poets, Lockhart's Scott, Mrs. Gaskell's Charlotte Bronte, Forster's Dickens, Trevelyan's Macaulay, Amy Lowell's Keats, the journals of Andre Gide, Shaw's letters to Ellen Terry, and the letters of Emily Dickinson.

The contribution made by political biography and autobiography to political history is evident from such titles as Beveridge's Life of John Marshall, Conyers Read's Mr. Secretary Walsingham, Catherine Bowen's Yankee from Olympus, Frances Perkins' The Roosevelt I Knew, Beatrice Webb's Our Partnership, such autobiographical writings as Jawaharlal Nehru's Toward Freedom, and the autobiographies of John Stuart Mill and Emma Goldman. To this group of political biographies one might also add the memoirs of Winston Churchill, the Intimate Papers of Col. House, and The Seven Pillars of Wisdom by Lawrence of Arabia.

Recent general interest in contemporary economic problems has brought with it a concurrent interest in the biography of economic figures. Here one might suggest Harrod's Life of John Maynard Keynes, or Count Harry Kessler's Walter Rathenau; His Life and Work, which has been characterized by Lewis Mumford as "a biographical appendix to Veblen's Theory of Business Enterprise, showing the conflict between pecuniary and technical standards in a single personality." Henry Ford's My Life and Work is almost unique as an autobiography of an industrial leader, a group which has not been notably introspective about its role in society. The biographical treatment of industrialists and financiers has tended to approach the extremes of either uncritical adoration in which Andrew Carnegie, the Goulds, James J. Hill, or William Randolph Hearst become humanitarians, public-spirited citizens, philanthropists, and lovers and patrons of the arts, or unabashed muckraking in which Rockefeller, Mellon, the Morgans, and the Du Ponts are vilified as leaders of a capitalism devoted to the perpetuation of a predatory feudalism. Here, too, one should mention Ida Tarbell's

History of the Standard Oil Company, not only because her work typifies the era of the muckrakers, but because this particular title is an early example of the history of a business enterprise, a type of biographical writing that has begun to gain increasing popularity -- the biography of the corporate personality.

In social biography the attention of the author is focussed upon the social environment of which he or his subject is a part, and hence it may be read either for casual observation of the minutiae of living, or for the substantial contribution it makes to the social history of a people or an age. The diaries of Pepys and Evelyn are classic examples of this kind of biographical writing, but more nearly contemporary social commentary is to be found in such consciously sociological writings as Jane Addams' Twenty Years at Hull House, Lincoln Steffens' Autobiography, Margaret Sanger's My Fight for Birth Control, Booker T. Washington's Up From Slavery, or Lauren Gilfillan's I Went to Pit College. The struggle of minority groups is poignantly recreated in Richard Wright's Black Boy, Rackham Holt's George Washington Carver, Ethel Waters' and Charles Samuels' His Eye is on the Sparrow, or Ludwig Lewisohn's Up Stream.

Similarly, autobiography may represent an intellectual excursion into the philosophic, mystical, or religious experiences of the individual. Here one may most readily distinguish such classic examples as John Bunyan's Grace Abounding, the Confessions of St. Augustine and Leo Tolstoy, the Journals of Emerson and Thoreau, and The Education of Henry Adams.

Biographical writing may also take the form of collective biography in which the lives of two or more individuals are set forth to explain or dramatize the spirit of an age. Thus Matthew Josephson's The Robber Barons castigates an era of uncontrolled capitalistic exploitation. Similar approaches to American history through the lives of selected central figures are to be found in Samuel Eliot Morison's Builders of the Bay Colony, or Gamaliel Bradford's Confederate Portraits, though the former is founded in a far more substantial scholarship. Lytton Strachey's Eminent Victorians is the same genre applied to English history of the late nineteenth century. A variation on this same technique is evinced by Ralph Roeder's The Man of the Renaissance, which is a composite portrait developed through study of typical figures of that age.

All biographical materials can contribute in greater or less degree to the study of psychology and heredity, but in recent decades there have appeared a number of biographical works that are overtly psychographic in approach. The forerunner of this school was Sir Edmund Gosse's Father and Son, which first appeared in 1908; and in this same category the two best known works of Lytton Strachey, Queen Victoria, and Elizabeth and Essex, are conspicuous examples of excellence. Literary figures, particularly, invite this kind of biographical appraisal, as witness Newton Arvin's Hawthorne, Van Wyck Brooks' The Ordeal of Mark Twain, or Joseph Wood Krutch's Edgar Allen Poe.

The distinction between biography and autobiography is only one of authorship and for the purposes of this discussion is not too meaningful, since autobiography as well as biography appears in any of the categories here set forth. Nevertheless, there are certain classic autobiographies that should be mentioned as landmark titles, and because they represent the highest development of the autobiographical art, e. g., the autobiographies of Mark Twain, Benjamin Franklin, and Benvenuto Cellini, The Education of Henry Adams, and H. G. Wells' Experiment in Autobiography. A special variety of autobiographical writing is that which relates to the years of the author's childhood and youth, including such titles as William Henry Hudson's Far Away and Long Ago, Tolstoy's Childhood and Youth, George Moore's Confessions of a Young Man, and Theodore Dreiser's History of Myself, of which the first volume is entitled Dawn.

An aberrant form of biography that has mushroomed into tremendous popularity in recent years is the humorous biography that focusses attention upon the queer character or funny family, and tends to be written about people of no particular importance except for their unorthodox behavior. The genesis of such writing may be Dickensian, but its immediate popularity probably stems from the success of Clarence Day's Life With Father, which is far more skillfully executed than most of its imitators. Nevertheless, A Genius in the Family, by Hiram Percy Maxim does make some slight contribution to social history, and Ruth McKenny's My Sister Eileen has a freshness that is lacking in many of the best-sellers in this class. To illustrate the merging of biography and fiction of this type, Betty Smith's A Tree Grows in Brooklyn might be cited.

Biographies of those who have gained eminence in the professions, specialized occupations, and other walks of life are almost limitless, and one can here name only a very few. Among biographies of scientists there are Harvey Cushing's Life of Sir William Osler, Eve Curie's Mme. Curie, and the Life and Letters of Charles Darwin. Among artists, one might mention Isadora Duncan's My Life, Romola Nijinsky's Nijinsky, George Arliss' Up the Years from Bloomsbury, Ernest Newman's monumental biography of Richard Wagner, and Alexander W. Thayer's no less notable biography of Beethoven, Giorgio Vasari's Lives of the Painters, first published in 1550, Thomas Hart Benton's An Artist in America, and Irving Stone's Lust for Life, a fictionalized biography of Vincent Van Gogh which played a rather important role in stimulating current enthusiasm for the artist and his work. Among biographies of teachers certainly Bliss Perry's And Gladly Teach is one of the best, and Wilbur L. Cross' Connecticut Yankee is as much a contribution to the political history of Connecticut during the years of his governorship as it is to the history of Yale, and the annals of American higher education.

The lives of librarians have not been made memorable by distinguished biographies. The American Library Pioneers volumes are uneven in quality, and usually strictly factual with little if any analysis or interpretation. Fielding H. Garrison's biography of John Shaw Billings is a scholarly treatment of the work of the distinguished librarian of the New York Public Library and founder of the Armed Forces Medical Library. Less labored in treatment and perhaps of equal interest to

122

librarians are such bibliophilic memorabilia as A. Edward Newton's This Book-Collecting Game, A. S. W. Rosenbach's Books and Bidders, and the bibliographical antiquarian tours of England, Scotland, France and Germany by Thomas Dibdin.

Taste in biography is always highly individual and it is not to be assumed that any reader will follow any one type exclusively. As a matter of fact, none of the categories mentioned here is discrete, nor are the titles cited intended to indicate either the best of their kind or those which would appeal to any one group of readers. The best selection policy for the general library is one of conscious catholicity, remembering always the great diversity of reader interest and the varying criteria of excellence.

Bibliographies of biography tend to be relatively short selected lists intended for special groups such as high school students, lists of "great" biographies, or lists of recent popular titles. Again, there are a few very useful bibliographies which serve as indexes to the contents of collective biographical works, the contents of which are seldom indicated through analytical entries in the catalog:

> Logasa, Hannah. Biography in collections suitable for junior and senior high schools. 3d ed. rev. and enl. N. Y.: Wilson, 1940. 152 pp.

> Riches, Phyllis M. An analytical bibliography of universal collected biography, comprising books published in the English tongue in Great Britain and Ireland, America and the British dominions ... London: Library Assn., 1934. 709 pp.

But perhaps the most interesting bibliographic type connected with biography is bio-bibliography, the listing of all the works of a particular individual. As early as the second century A. D., Galen, the author of more than five hundred works, found it necessary to complete two separate bibliographies in order to disclaim the many titles falsely attributed to him and to claim his own works. These two bibliographies, the first (De libris propriis liber) elaborately classified by topic in seventeen chapters, and the second (De ordine librorum suorum liber) which has survived only in a fragment, have been preserved for us in the 1525 edition of his collected works. [5] The Venerable Bede, in 731, appended his own autobibliography (Notitia de se ipso et de libris suis) to his Ecclesiastical History of Britain, and many of the early examples of general or subject bibliography were arranged as series of bio-bibliographies. [6] Today some of our finest examples of bibliographic scholarship are to be found in bio-bibliographic compilations, especially in the fields of literature and history. Thomas Jackson Holmes' three-volume bibli-

---

5

Besterman, op. cit. p. 3.

6

Ibid., p. 3.

ography of the writings of Cotton Mather (Cambridge: Harvard Universit, Press, 1940), and Allen T. Hazen's Bibliography of the Strawberry Hill Press (New Haven: Yale University Press, 1942), are outstanding examples of thorough scholarship. The work of The Bibliographical Society (British) and the American Bibliographical Society has promoted interest in the production of such compilations, and has done much to foster standards of accuracy and thoroughness in bibliographic description. These techniques differ markedly from standard library cataloging practice, the differences being the logical result of differences in purpose. Although these specialized bibliographic techniques are too complicated to discuss fully here, they are a fascinating and important field for further study on the part of those who are interested in scholarly humanistic librarianship.

Bibliography

Popular History (General)

Wells, H. G. The Outline of History. N. Y.: Macmillan, 1921.

Forbes, Esther. Paul Revere and the World he Lived in. Boston: Houghton Mifflin, 1942.

Schlesinger, Arthur M. jr. The Age of Jackson. Boston: Little, Brown, 1945.

Leech, Margaret. Reveille in Washington, 1860-1865. N. Y.: Harper, 1941.

Sullivan, Mark. Our Times: the United States, 1900-1925. N. Y.: Scribner, 1926-1935. 6 vols.

Allen, Frederick Lewis. Only Yesterday: an Informal History of the Nineteen-twenties. N. Y.: Harper, 1931.

History and the Child

Gray, Elizabeth. Adam of the Road. N. Y.: Viking, 1943.

Forbes, Esther. Johnny Tremaine. Boston: Houghton Mifflin, 1943.

Foster, Genevieve. George Washington's World. N. Y.: Scribner, 1941.

Field, Rachel. Hitty, Her First Hundred Years. N. Y.: Macmillan, 1929.

Historical Fiction

Muntz, Hope. The Golden Warrior. N. Y.: Scribner, 1949.

Dickens, Charles. A Tale of Two Cities. N. Y.: The Modern Library, 1935.

Hugo, Victor. Ninety-three. N. Y.: Harper, 1874.

Cannon, Le Grand. jr. Look to the Mountain. N. Y.: Holt, 1942.

Forbes, Esther. A Mirror for Witches. Boston: Houghton Mifflin, 1928.

_____. The Running of the Tide. Boston: Houghton Mifflin, 1946.

Benet, Stephen Vincent. John Brown's Body. N. Y.: Doubleday, 1928.

Biography

Asser, Bishop of Sherborne. Life of King Alfred. Oxford: The Clarendon Press, 1904.

Roeder, Ralph. The Man of the Renaissance. N. Y.: Viking, 1933.

Pepys, Samuel. Diary. N. Y.: Random House, 1946.

Morison, Samuel Eliot. Builders of the Bay Colony. Boston: Houghton Mifflin, 1930.

Thayer, Alexander W. Life of Ludwig van Beethoven. N. Y.: Beethoven Association, 1931. 3 vols.

Lowell, Amy. John Keats. Boston: Houghton Mifflin, 1925. 2 vols.

Thoreau, Henry David. Journal. ed. by Bradford Torrey. Boston: Houghton Mifflin, 1949. 14 vols.

Sandburg, Carl. Abraham Lincoln. N. Y.: Harcourt, Brace. 1926-1939. 6 vols.

Steffens, Lincoln. Autobiography. N. Y.: Harcourt, Brace, 1931.

Tarbell, Ida M. The History of the Standard Oil Company. N. Y.: McClure, Phillips, 1904.

Bowers, Claude. Beveridge and the Progressive Era. Boston: Houghton Mifflin, 1932.

Tolstoi, Lev N. Childhood, Boyhood, Youth. N. Y.: Crowell, 1899.

Wells, H. G. Experiment in Autobiography. N. Y.: Macmillan, 1934.

Perry, Bliss. And Gladly Teach. N. Y.: Houghton Mifflin, 1935.

Day, Clarence. Life with Father. N. Y.: Knopf, 1936.

Sherwood, Robert E. Roosevelt and Hopkins. N. Y.: Harper, 1948.

Roosevelt, Eleanor. This I Remember. N. Y.: Harper, 1949.

Harrod, Roy F. Life of John Maynard Keynes. London: Macmillan, 1951

DATE DUE